## BENCHMARK SERIES

Microsoft®

# PowerPoint®

## 365

### 2019 Edition

# Review and Assessment

**Nita Rutkosky** | **Audrey Roggenkamp**
Pierce College Puyallup
Puyallup, Washington
| **Ian Rutkosky**
Pierce College Puyallup
Puyallup, Washington

PARADIGM
EDUCATION SOLUTIONS

St. Paul

**Vice President, Content and Digital Solutions:** Christine Hurney
**Director of Content Development:** Carley Fruzetti
**Developmental Editor:** Jennifer Joline Anderson
**Director of Production:** Timothy W. Larson
**Production Editor/Project Manager:** Jen Weaverling
**Senior Design and Production Specialist:** Jack Ross
**Cover and Interior Design:** Valerie King
**Copy Editor:** Communicáto, Ltd.
**Testers:** Janet Blum, Angela Niño, Lisa Hart
**Indexer:** Terry Casey
**Vice President, Director of Digital Products:** Chuck Bratton
**Digital Projects Manager:** Tom Modl
**Digital Solutions Manager:** Gerry Yumul
**Senior Director of Digital Products and Onboarding:** Christopher Johnson
**Supervisor of Digital Products and Onboarding:** Ryan Isdahl
**Vice President, Marketing:** Lara Weber McLellan
**Marketing and Communications Manager:** Selena Hicks

**Cover Photo Credit:** © lowball-jack/GettyImages

ISBN 978-0-76388-735-3 (print)
ISBN 978-0-76388-711-7 (digital)

© 2020 by Paradigm Publishing, LLC
875 Montreal Way
St. Paul, MN 55102
Email: CustomerService@ParadigmEducation.com
Website: ParadigmEducation.com

Printed in the United States of America

28 27 26 25 24 23 22 21 20 19     1 2 3 4 5 6 7 8 9 10 11 12

# Contents

# PowerPoint®

# Unit 1

## Creating and Formatting Presentations

# Preparing a PowerPoint Presentation

 The online course includes additional review and assessment resources.

## Skills Assessment

Assessment

1

### Create a Presentation on Types of Resumes

1. Create a presentation with the text shown in Figure 1.1 on the next page by completing the following steps:
   a. With PowerPoint open, click the *New* option at the PowerPoint opening screen or click the File tab and then click the *New* option.
   b. At the New backstage area, click the *Wood Type* design theme template, click the color variant in the second column, top row, and then click the Create button.
   c. Create slides with the text shown in Figure 1.1. Use the Title Slide layout for slides 1 and 5 and use the Title and Content layout for slides 2, 3, and 4.
2. Save the completed presentation in the PC1 folder on your storage medium with the name **1-ResumeTypes**.
3. Apply the Push slide transition (in the *Subtle* section) with a From Left effect to all slides in the presentation.
4. Change the transition duration for all slides to 01.50 seconds.
5. Apply the Wind transition sound to all slides in the presentation.
6. Run the slide show.
7. Print the presentation as a handout with six slides displayed horizontally per page.
8. Save and then close **1-ResumeTypes**.

**Figure 1.1** Assessment 1

| | | | |
|---|---|---|---|
| Slide 1 | Title | = | Career Finders |
| | Subtitle | = | Types of Resumes |
| Slide 2 | Title | = | Functional Resume |
| | Bullets | = | ▪ Emphasizes skills and achievements |
| | | | ▪ Used when you lack a formal education |
| | | | ▪ Used when you have had many different jobs with no clear pattern or progression |
| Slide 3 | Title | = | Chronological Resume |
| | Bullets | = | ▪ List more recent training or jobs first and then proceed backwards |
| | | | ▪ Components include: |
| | | | ▪ Personal contact information |
| | | | ▪ Employment history |
| | | | ▪ Educational qualifications |
| | | | ▪ Professional development |
| Slide 4 | Title | = | Hybrid Resume |
| | Bullets | = | ▪ Combines best of chronological and functional resume |
| | | | ▪ Contains fixed order of chronological resume |
| | | | ▪ More emphasis on skills and achievements |
| Slide 5 | Title | = | Career Finders |
| | Subtitle | = | Sign up today for Career Finders resume writing workshop! |

**Assessment 2**

## Create a Presentation on Preparing a Company Newsletter

1. At a blank screen, click the File tab and then click the *New* option.
2. At the New backstage area, click the *Blank Presentation* template.
3. Create slides with the text shown in Figure 1.2.
4. Apply the Basis design theme and the orange color variant (third option in the Variants group).
5. Run the slide show.
6. Print the presentation as a handout with all six slides displayed horizontally per page.
7. Make the following changes to the presentation:
   a. Apply the Parallax design theme and the red color variant (fourth option in the Variants group).
   b. Add the Switch transition (in the *Exciting* section) with a Left effect to all slides.
   c. Add the Camera transition sound to all slides.
   d. Specify that all slides advance automatically after five seconds.
8. Run the slide show.
9. Save the presentation and name it **1-Newsletter**.
10. Close **1-Newsletter**.

**Figure 1.2** Assessment 2

| | | | |
|---|---|---|---|
| Slide 1 | Title | = | Preparing a Company Newsletter |
| | Subtitle | = | Planning and Designing the Layout |

Slide 2    Title   =    Planning a Newsletter

         Bullets   =
- Use pictures of different people from your organization in each issue.
- Distribute contributor sheets soliciting information from employees.
- Keep the focus of the newsletter on issues of interest to employees.

Slide 3    Title   =    Planning a Newsletter

         Bullets   =
- Focus on various levels of employment
- Conduct regular surveys to provide updated information

Slide 4    Title   =    Designing a Newsletter

         Bulllets   =
- Maintain consistent elements from issue to issue such as:
  - Column layout
  - Nameplate formatting and location
  - Formatting of headlines
  - Use of color

Slide 5    Title   =    Designing a Newsletter

         Bullets   =
- Consider the following elements when designing a newsletter:
  - Focus
  - Balance
  - White space
  - Directional flow

Slide 6    Title   =    Creating a Newsletter Layout

         Bullets   =
- Choose paper size
- Choose paper weight
- Determine margins
- Specify column layout

# Visual Benchmark

## Create a Presentation on Job Interview Tips and Strategies

1. Create the presentation shown in Figure 1.3 on the next page with the following specifications:
   a. Apply the Organic design theme template and the appropriate color variant.
   b. Create six slides as shown in the figure.
   c. Apply a transition, transition sound, and transition duration time of your choosing to each slide in the presentation.
2. Save the completed presentation and name it **1-Interview**.
3. Run the slide show.
4. Print the presentation as a handout with all six slides displayed horizontally per page.
5. Close the presentation.

# Case Study

**Part 1**

You work for Citizens for Consumer Safety, a nonprofit organization providing information on household safety. Your supervisor, Melinda Johansson, will be presenting information on smoke detectors at a community meeting and has asked you to prepare a PowerPoint presentation. Open the Word document named **PPSmokeDetectors** from your PC1 folder. Read over the information and then use it to prepare a presentation containing at least five slides. Also refer to Chapter 1, page 9, for guidelines on planning a presentation. Apply an appropriate design theme and add a transition and transition sound to all slides. Save the presentation and name it **1-PPSmokeDetectors**. Run the slide show and then print the presentation as a handout with all slides on one page.

**Part 2**

Ms. Johansson has looked at the printout of the presentation and has asked you to print another copy in grayscale, with two slides per page. Explore options at the Print backstage area to learn how to print in grayscale and then print one copy of the presentation in grayscale with two slides per page.

**Part 3**

As part of the presentation, Ms. Johansson would like to provide information about where to purchase smoke detectors online. Using the internet, locate at least three sites that sell smoke detectors. Insert a new slide in **1-PPSmokeDetectors** that includes the names of the stores, web addresses, and any additional information you feel is important, such as models and pricing. Save the presentation and then print a copy in Outline view. Close the presentation.

**Figure 1.3** Visual Benchmark

Slide 1

Slide 2

Slide 3

Slide 4

Slide 5

Slide 6

# Modifying a Presentation and Using Help and Tell Me

 The online course includes additional review and assessment resources.

## Skills Assessment

**Assessment**

**1**

### Create an Electronic Design Presentation

1. Use the outline shown in Figure 2.1 to create a presentation using the Wisp design theme and the second color variant. (When typing bulleted text, press the Tab key to move the insertion point to the next tab level.)
2. After creating the slides, complete a spelling check on the text in the slides.
3. Save the presentation in your PC2 folder and name it **2-ElecDesign**.
4. Run the slide show.
5. Print the presentation as a handout with four slides displayed horizontally per page.
6. Make the following changes to the presentation:
    a. Change to Slide Sorter view and then move Slide 3 (*Creating Focus*) between Slides 1 and 2.
    b. Move Slide 4 (*Providing Proportion*) between Slides 2 and 3.
    c. Change to Normal view.
    d. Search for the word *document* and replace it with the word *brochure*. (After the replacements, make Slide 1 active and, if necessary, capitalize the "b" in *brochure*.)
    e. Apply the Uncover transition and Hammer transition sound to each slide.
7. Save the presentation.
8. Display the Reuse Slides task pane, browse to your PC2 folder, and then double-click *LayoutTips*.
9. Insert the *Layout Punctuation Tips* slide below Slide 4.
10. Insert the *Layout Tips* slide below Slide 5.
11. Close the Reuse Slides task pane.
12. Find all occurrences of *Layout* and replace with *Design*. (Insert a check mark in the *Match case* check box.)
13. Move Slide 5 (*Design Punctuation Tips*) between Slides 1 and 2.
14. Move Slide 6 (*Design Tips*) between Slides 2 and 3.
15. Save the presentation.
16. Print the presentation as a handout with six slides displayed horizontally per page.
17. Beginning with Slide 2 (*Design Punctuation Tips*), create a section named *Design Tips*.
18. Beginning with Slide 4 (*Creating Focus*), create a section named *Design Features*.
19. Print only the Design Features section as a handout with four slides displayed horizontally per page.
20. Save and then close **2-ElecDesign**.

**Figure 2.1** Assessment 1

| | | | |
|---|---|---|---|
| Slide I | Title | = | Electronic Design and Production |
| | Subtitle | = | Designing a Document |

Slide 2  Title  =  Creating Balance
         Bullets  =  • Symmetrical balance: Balancing similar elements equally on a page (centered alignment) of the document
                     • Asymmetrical balance: Balancing contrasting elements on a page of the document

Slide 3  Title  =  Creating Focus
         Bullets  =  • Creating focus with titles, headings, and subheads in a document
                     • Creating focus with graphic elements in a document
                       ○ Images
                       ○ Watermarks
                       ○ Charts
                       ○ Graphs

Slide 4  Title  =  Providing Proportion
         Bullets  =  • Evaluating proportions in a document
                     • Sizing graphic elements in a document
                     • Using white space in a document

## Assessment 2

### Create a Netiquette Presentation

1. Create a presentation with the text shown in Figure 2.2. You determine the slide layout. Apply the Organic design theme and the fourth color variant.
2. If necessary, size and move placeholders so the text is positioned attractively on the slide.
3. Select Slides 4 through 6 and then duplicate the slides.
4. Type the following text in place of the existing text in the identified slides:
   a. Slide 7: Select the netiquette rule text in the subtitle placeholder and then type Do not plagiarize.
   b. Slide 8: Select the netiquette rule text in the subtitle placeholder and then type Respect and accept people's differences.
   c. Slide 9: Select the netiquette rule text in the subtitle placeholder and then type Respect others' time.
5. Complete a spelling check on the text in the presentation.
6. Save the presentation and name it **2-InternetApps**.
7. Print the presentation as a handout with six slides displayed horizontally per page.
8. Make the following edits to the presentation:
   a. Display the presentation in Slide Sorter view.
   b. Move Slide 3 between Slide 5 and Slide 6.
   c. Move Slide 7 between Slide 3 and Slide 4.

**Figure 2.2** Assessment 2

| | | | |
|---|---|---|---|
| Slide 1 | Title | = | CONNECTING ONLINE |
| | Subtitle | = | Internet Applications |
| Slide 2 | Title | = | Internet Community |
| | Bullets | = | • Email |
| | | | • Internet voice services |
| | | | • Moderated environments |
| | | | • Netiquette |
| Slide 3 | Title | = | Netiquette Rule |
| | Subtitle | = | Remember you are dealing with people. |
| Slide 4 | Title | = | Netiquette Rule |
| | Subtitle | = | Adhere to the same standards of behavior online that you follow in real life. |
| Slide 5 | Title | = | Netiquette Rule |
| | Subtitle | = | Respect the privacy of others. |
| Slide 6 | Title | = | Netiquette Rule |
| | Subtitle | = | Share expert knowledge. |

9. Apply the Split transition, the Click transition sound, and change the duration to 01.00 second for all slides in the presentation.
10. Save the presentation and then run the slide show.
11. Print the presentation as a handout with nine slides displayed horizontally per page.
12. Close **2-InternetApps**.

## Assessment 3

### Download a Design Theme

1. If your computer is connected to the internet, you can search online for design themes you can download to your computer. Display the New backstage area, click in the search text box, type digital blue tunnel presentation, and then press the Enter key.
2. Click the *Business digital blue tunnel presentation (widescreen)* template (all of the template name may not be visible) and then click the Create button. (If the *Business digital blue tunnel presentation (widescreen)* template is not available, open **DigitalBlue** from your PC2 folder.)
3. When the design theme is downloaded and a presentation is opened with the design theme applied, select and then delete the eleven slides in the presentation.
4. Open **2-InternetApps**.
5. Select the nine slides in the **2-InternetApps** file and then click the Copy button.

6. Position the mouse pointer on the PowerPoint button on the taskbar and then click the thumbnail representing the presentation with the downloaded design theme.
7. Click the Paste button to paste the nine slides in the current presentation.
8. Scroll through and look at each slide and, if necessary, make any changes required so the text is positioned attractively on each slide.
9. Save the presentation and name it **2-ConnectOnline**.
10. Run the slide show.
11. Print the presentation as a handout with nine slides displayed horizontally per page.
12. Close **2-ConnectOnline** and then close **2-InternetApps**.

# Visual Benchmark

## Format a Presentation on Online Learning

1. Open **OnlineLearn** and then save it with the name **2-OnlineLearn**.
2. Format the presentation so it appears as shown in Figure 2.3 on the next page with the following specifications:
   a. Apply the Parallax design theme and the fourth color variant.
   b. Use the Reuse Slides task pane to insert the two additional slides from the **Learning** presentation.
   c. Arrange the slides to match what you see in Figure 2.3. (Read the slides from left to right.)
   d. Size and/or move placeholders so text displays in each slide as shown in Figure 2.3.
3. Add a transition and transition sound of your choosing to each slide.
4. Run the slide show.
5. Print the presentation as a handout with six slides displayed horizontally per page.
6. Save and then close **2-OnlineLearn**.

**Figure 2.3** Visual Benchmark

Slide 1

Slide 2

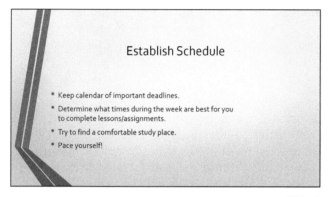

Slide 3

Slide 4

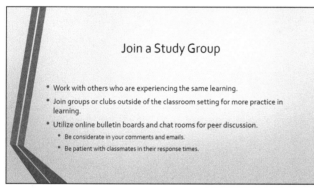

Slide 5

Slide 6

# Case Study

**Part 1**

You are the office manager at the Career Finders agency. One of your responsibilities is to conduct workshops to prepare individuals for the job search process. A coworker has given you a presentation for the workshop but the presentation needs some editing and modifying. Open **JobAnalysis** and then save it with the name **2-JobAnalysis**. Check each slide in the presentation and then make modifications to maintain consistency in the size and location of placeholders (consider using the Reset button to reset the formatting and size of the placeholders), maintain consistency in heading text, move text from an overcrowded slide to a new slide, complete a spelling check, apply a design theme, and make any other modifications to improve the presentation. Save **2-JobAnalysis**.

**Part 2**

After reviewing the presentation, you realize that you need to include slides on resumes. Open **ResumePres** and then copy Slides 2 and 3 into **2-JobAnalysis** (at the end of the presentation). You want to add additional information on resume writing tips and decide to use the internet to find information. Search for tips on writing a resume and then create a slide (or two) with the information you find. Add a transition and transition sound to all slides in the presentation. Save **2-JobAnalysis**.

**Part 3**

You know that Microsoft Word offers a number of online resume templates that can be downloaded. You decide to include information in the presentation on how to find and download resumes. Open Microsoft Word and, at the Word opening screen, click the *New* option, click in the search text box, type resume, and then press the Enter key. Scroll through the list of resume templates and then experiment with downloading a template. With **2-JobAnalysis** open, add an additional slide to the end of the presentation that provides steps on how to download a resume in Microsoft Word. Print the presentation as a handout with six slides displayed horizontally per page. Run the slide show. Save and then close the presentation.

**CHAPTER**

**3**

# Formatting Slides

 The online course includes additional review and assessment resources.

## Skills Assessment

**Assessment**

**1**

### Create, Format, and Modify a Benefits Presentation

1. Open a new, blank presentation and create five slides as outlined in Figure 3.1.
2. Apply the Facet design theme and then apply the blue variant.
3. Make Slide 1 active and then make the following changes:
   a. Select the title *BENEFITS PROGRAM*; change the font to Candara and the font size to 60 points; apply the Turquoise, Accent 1, Darker 50% font color (fifth column, last row in the *Theme Colors* section); and apply italic formatting.
   b. Select the subtitle *Changes to Plans*; change the font to Candara and the font size to 32 points; apply the Turquoise, Accent 1 font color (fifth column, first row in the *Theme Colors* section); and apply bold and shadow formatting.
   c. Center the title in the placeholder.
   d. Center the subtitle in the placeholder.
4. Make Slide 2 active and then make the following changes:
   a. Select the title *INTRODUCTION*; change the font to Candara and the font size to 44 points; apply the Turquoise, Accent 1, Darker 50% font color; and apply shadow formatting.
   b. Using Format Painter, apply the formatting set in Step 4a to the titles in the remaining slides.
5. Center-align and middle-align the titles in Slides 2 through 5.
6. Make Slide 2 active, select the placeholder containing the bulleted text (make sure the placeholder border displays as a solid line), and then change the line spacing to double spacing (2.0).
7. Make Slide 3 active, select the placeholder containing the bulleted text, and then change the line spacing to double spacing (2.0).
8. Make Slide 4 active, select the placeholder containing the bulleted text, and then change the line spacing to 1.5 lines.
9. Make Slide 5 active, select the placeholder containing the bulleted text, and then change the spacing after paragraphs to 18 points. ***Hint: Do this at the Paragraph dialog box.***
10. Make Slide 2 active and then select the placeholder containing the bulleted text. Display the Bullets and Numbering dialog box with the Numbered tab selected; click the *1. 2. 3.* option; change the size to 90%; apply the Turquoise, Accent 1, Darker 50% color; and then close the dialog box.

11. Make Slide 3 active and then select the placeholder containing the bulleted text. Display the Bullets and Numbering dialog box with the Numbered tab selected; click the *1. 2. 3.* option; change the size to 90%; apply the Turquoise, Accent 1, Darker 50% color, change the starting number to 5; and then close the dialog box.
12. Make Slide 4 active, select the placeholder containing the bulleted text, and then change the bullets to the Hollow Square Bullets style.
13. Make Slide 5 active, select the placeholder containing the bulleted text, and then change the bullets to the Hollow Square Bullets style.
14. Save the presentation and name it **3-Benefits**.
15. Print the presentation as a handout with six slides displayed horizontally per page.
16. Apply the Organic design theme.
17. Apply a transition and transition sound of your choosing to each slide.
18. Run the slide show.
19. Print the presentation as a handout with six slides displayed horizontally per page.
20. Save and then close **3-Benefits**.

**Figure 3.1** Assessment 1

| Slide 1 | Title | = | BENEFITS PROGRAM |
| | Subtitle | = | Changes to Plans |
| Slide 2 | Title | = | INTRODUCTION |
| | Content | = | • Changes made for 2021 |
| | | | • Description of eligibility |
| | | | • Instructions for enrolling new members |
| | | | • Overview of medical and dental coverage |
| Slide 3 | Title | = | INTRODUCTION |
| | Content | = | • Expanded enrollment forms |
| | | | • Glossary defining terms |
| | | | • Telephone directory |
| | | | • Pamphlet with commonly asked questions |
| Slide 4 | Title | = | WHAT'S NEW |
| | Content | = | • New medical plans |
| | | | ○ Plan 2021 |
| | | | ○ Premier Plan |
| | | | • Changes in monthly contributions |
| | | | • Paying with pretax dollars |
| | | | • Contributions toward spouse's coverage |
| Slide 5 | Title | = | COST SHARING |
| | Content | = | • Increased deductible |
| | | | • New coinsurance amount |
| | | | • Co-payment for mail-order medicines |
| | | | • New stop loss limit |

## Format and Modify a Perennials Presentation

1. Open **PerennialsPres** and then save it with the name **3-PerennialsPres**.
2. Make Slide 3 active, select the placeholder containing the bulleted text, format the bulleted text into two columns, and change the line spacing to double spacing (2.0). Make sure each column contains four bulleted items. With the placeholder selected, display the Paragraph dialog box, change the *By* option (in the *Indentation* section) to 0.4 inch, and then close the dialog box.
3. Make Slide 2 active, select the placeholder containing the bulleted text, click the Drawing group task pane launcher, and then make the following changes at the Format Shape task pane:
   a. With the Fill & Line icon selected, click *Fill* to expand the options; click the *Gradient fill* option; use the *Type* option to change to Rectangular; use the Color button to apply the Green, Accent 1, Lighter 60% color (fifth column, third row in the *Theme Colors* section); and then make sure *0%* displays in the *Position* measurement box (located below the Color button).
   b. Click the Effects icon, click the *Shadow* option, click the Presets button, and then click the *Offset: Right* option (first column, second row).
   c. Click the Size & Properties icon and then click *Text Box* to display the options.
   d. Change the left margin measurement to 1 inch and the top margin measurement to 0.4 inch.
   e. Close the task pane.
4. Make Slide 1 active, click the subtitle placeholder, and then apply the following shape and outline fill:
   a. Click the Shape Fill button arrow on the Home tab and then click the *Eyedropper* option.
   b. Point the eyedropper to the light green border at the top of the slide and then click the left mouse button.
   c. Click the Shape Outline button arrow and then click the *Eyedropper* option.
   d. Position the tip of the eyedropper on a yellow colored flower in the Greenspace Architects logo and then click the left mouse button.
5. Make Slide 2 active, click the Design tab, click the Format Background button, and then apply the following formatting:
   a. At the Format Background task pane with the Fill icon selected, click the *Solid fill* option.
   b. Click the Color button and then click the *Dark Green, Text 2, Lighter 80%* option (fourth column, second row in the *Theme Colors* section).
   c. Click the Apply to All button.
   d. Close the task pane.
6. Print the presentation with six slides displayed horizontally per page.
7. Add a transition and transition sound of your choosing to all slides in the presentation.
8. Run the slide show.
9. Save and then close **3-PerennialsPres**.

## Create and Apply a Custom Design Theme to a Travel Presentation

1. Open a new, blank presentation and apply the Parallax design theme.
2. Create custom theme colors named with your first and last names that changes the following colors:
   a. At the Create New Theme Colors dialog box, change the Text/Background - Light 2 color to Red, Accent 4, Lighter 80% (eighth column, second row in the *Theme Colors* section).

b. Change the Accent 1 color to Red, Accent 4, Darker 50% (eighth column, last row in the *Theme Colors* section).

3. Create custom theme fonts named with your first and last names that changes the Heading font to Copperplate Gothic Bold and the Body font to Rockwell.

4. Save the current design theme as a custom design theme named with your first and last names. ***Hint: Do this at the Save Current Theme dialog box.***

5. Close the presentation without saving it.

6. Open **TravelEngland** and then save it with the name **3-TravelEngland**.

7. Apply the custom design theme you just created named with your first and last names.

8. Improve the visual display of the bulleted text in Slides 2 and 3 by increasing the spacing between items and positioning the bulleted item placeholders attractively in the slides.

9. Make Slide 4 active, increase the spacing between the bulleted items and then format the text into two columns. Make sure that each column contains three bulleted items.

10. Format the bulleted text in Slides 5 and 6 into two columns with four bulleted items in each column.

11. Print the presentation as a handout with six slides displayed horizontally per page.

12. Add a transition and transition sound of your choosing to all slides in the presentation.

13. Run the slide show.

14. Save and then close **3-TravelEngland**.

15. Display a blank presentation and then delete the custom theme colors, custom theme fonts, and custom design theme you created for this assessment.

16. Close the presentation without saving it.

## Assessment 4

### Prepare a Presentation on Online Shopping

1. Open Word and then open **OnlineShopping** from your PC3 folder. Print the document by clicking the File tab, clicking the *Print* option, and then clicking the Print button at the Print backstage area.

2. Close **OnlineShopping** and then close Word.

3. Open a blank PowerPoint presentation and use the information you printed to create a presentation on online shopping with the following specifications:
   a. Create a slide with the title of your presentation. Type your name as the subtitle.
   b. Create slides that summarize the information you printed. (You determine the number of slides in the presentation. Make sure the slides are not too crowded with information.)
   c. Apply a design theme of your choosing.
   d. Apply a transition and transition sound of your choosing to all slides.

4. Save the presentation and name it **3-OnlineShopping**.

5. Run the slide show.

6. Print the presentation as a handout with six slides displayed horizontally per page.

7. Close **3-OnlineShopping**.

# Visual Benchmark

## Format a Presentation on Home Safety

1. Open **HomeSafety** and then save it with the name **3-HomeSafety**.
2. Format the presentation so the slides appear as shown in Figure 3.2 with the following specifications:
   a. Apply the Facet design theme and the blue variant color.
   b. Delete and rearrange slides as shown in the figure.
   c. Apply the Parchment texture slide background and change the slide background transparency to 50% for all slides in the presentation. ***Hint: Apply these options using the Format Background task pane.***
   d. Change the font size of the title in Slide 1 to 60 points; apply bold formatting; apply the Blue, Accent 2, Darker 25% font color (sixth column, fifth row in the *Theme Colors* section); and center-align the title.
   e. Change the font size of the subtitle in Slide 1 to 28 points; apply italic formatting; change the font color to Turquoise, Accent 1, Darker 25% (fifth column, fifth row in the *Theme Colors* section); and center-align the subtitle.
   f. Change the font size of the titles in Slides 2 through 6 to 48 points and the font color to Turquoise, Accent 1, Darker 50% (fifth column, last row in the *Theme Colors* section).
   g. Change the line spacing, spacing after, column formatting, and bullet styles so your slides look similar to the slides in Figure 3.2.
   h. Select the bulleted text placeholder in Slide 6; display the Format Shape task pane; click the *Solid fill* option; and then change the color to Turquoise, Accent 1, Lighter 80% (fifth column, second row in the *Theme Colors* section). Click the Size & Properties icon, click the *Text Box* option, and then change the left margin to 1 inch and the top margin to 0.2 inches.
3. Run the slide show.
4. Print the presentation as a handout with six slides displayed horizontally per page.
5. Save and then close the presentation.

**Figure 3.2** Visual Benchmark

Slide 1

Slide 2

Slide 3

Slide 4

Slide 5

Slide 6

# Case Study

Part

1

You are the assistant to Gina Coletti, manager of La Dolce Vita, an Italian restaurant. She has been working on a new lunch menu and wants to present the new menu at the upcoming staff meeting. She has asked you to prepare a presentation she can use at the meeting. Open Word, open the Word document named **LunchMenu** from your PC3 folder, and then print the document. Close the document and then close Word. In PowerPoint, display the New backstage area, search online for the *Fresh food presentation* design theme template, and then download the template that contains the vegetables on the title slide. (If the *Fresh food presentation* template is not available, open **FreshFood** from your PC3 folder.) Select and then delete slides 2 through 11. Create a presentation with the design theme template you downloaded and the information you printed. Make any formatting changes you feel are necessary to improve the appearance of the presentation. Save the presentation and name it **3-LunchMenu**.

Part

2

Ms. Coletti has looked over the presentation and has asked you to apply color and font formatting consistent with the other restaurant publications. With **3-LunchMenu** open, create custom theme colors that change the Text/Background - Light 1 color to Gold, Accent 2, Lighter 80% (sixth column, second row in the *Theme Colors* section) and the Accent 3 color to Blue (eighth option in the *Standard Colors* section). Create custom theme fonts that apply Monotype Corsiva as the heading font and Garamond as the body font. Save the custom theme and name it *LaDolceVita* followed by your initials. Add a transition and transition sound to all slides in the presentation. Print the presentation as a handout with six slides displayed horizontally per page. Save and then close **3-LunchMenu**.

Part

3

Ms. Coletti needs additional information for the meeting. She wants you to use the internet to search for two companies that print restaurant menus, two companies that design restaurant menus, and the names of two restaurant menu design software programs. Prepare a presentation with the information you find on the internet using the design theme template you downloaded in part 1. Make any formatting changes to improve the appearance of each slide. Add a transition and transition sound to each slide in the presentation. Save the presentation and name it **3-RestMenus**. Print the presentation as a handout with six slides displayed horizontally per page.

Part

4

When running **3-RestMenus**, Ms. Coletti would like to link to a couple of the sites you list in the presentation. Use PowerPoint's Help feature to learn how to insert a hyperlink in a slide to a web page or website. Create at least two hyperlinks between sites you list in the presentation and the web page or website. Run the slide show and click the hyperlinks to view the websites. Print the slide(s) containing the hyperlinks. Save and then close **3-RestMenus**.

CHAPTER

# 4

# Inserting Elements in Slides

 The online course includes additional review and assessment resources.

## Skills Assessment

Assessment
1

### Format and Add Enhancements to a Travel Presentation

1. Open **TravelEngland** and then save it with the name **4-TravelEngland**.
2. Make Slide 8 active and then insert the slide shown in Figure 4.1 (on page 25) with the following specifications:
   a. Insert a new slide with the Title Only layout.
   b. Type the title *Travel England* as shown in the slide.
   c. Draw a text box in the slide and then type the text shown in Figure 4.1. Select and then change the text font size to 40 points and apply the Tan, Background 2, Darker 75% font color (third column, fifth row in the *Theme Colors* section).
   d. Apply the Tan, Background 2, Darker 10% shape fill (third column, second row in the *Theme Colors* section) to the text box.
   e. Apply the Glow: 8 point; Dark Teal, Accent color 4 shape effect (fourth column, second row in the *Glow* side menu).
   f. Display the Format Shape task pane with the Size & Properties icon selected, change the height to 2.8 inches and the width to 9 inches (in the *Size* section). Change the left, right, top, and bottom margins to 0.4 inch (in the *Text Box* section). Close the Format Shape task pane.
   g. Distribute the text box horizontally and vertically on the slide. (Do this with the Align button on the Drawing Tools Format tab.)
3. Make Slide 2 active, select the text in the text box and then set a left tab at the 0.5-inch mark on the horizontal ruler, a center tab at the 6-inch mark, and a right tab at the 9.5-inch mark. Bold the headings in the first row.
4. Make Slide 6 active, select the image, and then make the following changes:
   a. Use the Corrections button on the Picture Tools Format tab to sharpen the image by 25% (fourth option in the *Sharpen/Soften* section).
   b. Display the Format Picture task pane with the Size & Properties icon selected.
   c. Change the scale height to 150%, the horizontal position to 5.5 inches, the vertical position to 2.2 inches, and then close the task pane.
5. Make Slide 4 active and then insert the **Stonehenge** image from your PC4 folder with the following specifications:
   a. Crop the image so it displays as shown in Figure 4.2 (on page 25).
   b. Type Photograph of Stonehenge as alternative text for the image at the Alt Text task pane.

c. Send the image behind the text.

d. Size and move the image so it displays as shown in Figure 4.2.

e. Size and move the bulleted text placeholder so it displays as shown in Figure 4.2.

6. Make Slide 7 active and then insert the **Umbrella** image from your PC4 folder with the following specifications (see Figure 4.3 on page 26):

a. Flip the umbrella horizontally. (Do this with the Rotate button.)

b. Correct the image to Brightness: -40% Contrast: +20% (first column, fourth row in the *Brightness/Contrast* section).

c. Change the height of the image to 4 inches.

d. Change the horizontal position to 6.8 inches and the vertical position to 2 inches at the Format Picture task pane with the Size & Properties icon selected.

7. Make Slide 8 active, display the Format Background task pane (use the Format Background button on the Design tab), and insert the image shown in Figure 4.4 (on page 26) with the following specifications:

a. Insert the image with the File button in the Format Background task pane with the Fill icon selected and the *Picture or texture fill* option selected. The image is named **StonehengeSunset** and is in your PC4 folder.

b. With the Fill icon selected in the Format Background task pane, change the *Offset left* option to -10% and the *Offset right* option to -3%.

c. Click the Picture icon in the Format Background task pane and then change the contrast to 30%. Close the Format Background task pane.

d. Change the font color of the subtitle *Wiltshire - The Heart of Wessex* to Lime, Accent 3, Lighter 40% (seventh column, fourth row in the *Theme Colors* section).

e. Size and move the text in placeholders so the text is positioned as shown in Figure 4.4.

8. Make Slide 9 active and then insert a new slide with the Title Only layout. Insert the title and insert and format a shape as shown in Figure 4.5 (on page 27) with the following specifications:

a. Type the title *Travel Discounts!* as shown in Figure 4.5.

b. Draw the shape shown in the slide using the Scroll: Horizontal shape (sixth column, second row in the *Stars and Banners* section).

c. Change the height of the shape to 5 inches and the width to 10 inches.

d. Apply the Subtle Effect - Dark Teal, Accent 4 shape style to the shape (fifth column, fourth row).

e. Type the text in the shape as shown in the figure. Change the font size for the text to 36 points; apply the Tan, Background 2, Darker 75% font color (third column, fifth row in the *Theme Colors* section), and then apply bold formatting.

f. Distribute the shape horizontally and vertically on the slide.

9. Apply the Peel Off transition to each slide.

10. Insert slide numbers on each slide.

11. Insert a footer for notes and handouts pages that prints your first and last names.

12. Run the slide show.

13. Print the presentation as a handout with six slides displayed horizontally per page.

14. Save and then close **4-TravelEngland**.

**Figure 4.1** Assessment 1, Step 2

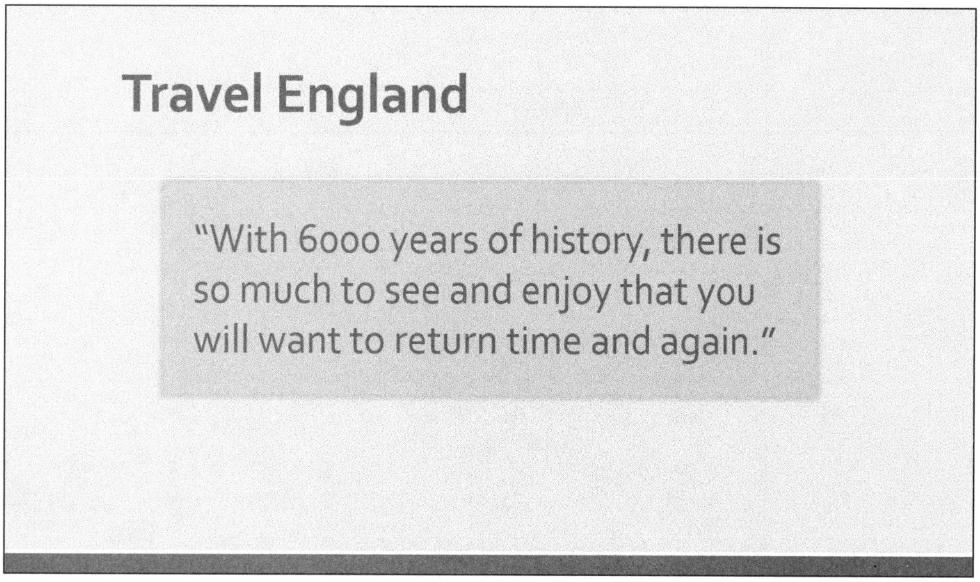

**Travel England**

"With 6000 years of history, there is so much to see and enjoy that you will want to return time and again."

**Figure 4.2** Assessment 1, Step 5

**Ancient Stone Circles**

- Stonehenge
- Avebury
- The Sanctuary

**Figure 4.3** Assessment 1, Step 6

**Figure 4.4** Assessment 1, Step 7

**Figure 4.5** Assessment 1, Step 8

## Assessment 2

### Format and Add Enhancements to a Gardening Presentation

1. Open **Greenspace** and then save it with the name **4-Greenspace**.
2. Insert the slide shown in Figure 4.6 (on page 29) with the following specifications:
   a. Make Slide 2 active and then insert a new slide with the Blank layout.
   b. Insert a WordArt text box using the option in the second column, bottom row (gold fill with horizontal stripes) and then type Think Spring! as the WordArt text.
   c. Change the shape of the WordArt to Wave: Down. (The *Wave: Down* option is the first option in the fifth row in the *Warp* section of the Text Effects button *Transform* side menu.)
   d. Change the height of the WordArt to 4 inches and the width to 10 inches.
   e. Distribute the WordArt horizontally and vertically on the slide.
   f. Display the Format Background task pane. (Display this task pane by clicking the Format Background button on the Design tab.) Insert a check mark in the *Hide background graphics* check box. Click the Preset gradients button, click the *Light Gradient - Accent 3* option (third column, first row), and then close the task pane.
3. Insert the slide shown in Figure 4.7 (on page 29) with the following specifications:
   a. Make Slide 8 active and then insert a new slide with the Title Only layout.
   b. Insert the title *English/French Translations* as shown in Figure 4.7.
   c. Insert a text box, change the font size to 28 points, set left tabs at the 1-inch and the 5.5-inch marks on the horizontal ruler, and then type the text shown in Figure 4.7 in columns. Bold the headings *English Name* and *French Name* and use the Symbol dialog box to insert the special symbols in the French names. Use the (normal text) font at the Symbol dialog box to insert the symbols.
   d. If necessary, move the text box so it is positioned as shown in Figure 4.7.
4. Make Slide 4 active and then make the following changes:
   a. Select the bulleted text and then change the line spacing to double spacing (2.0).

b. With the bulleted text selected, format the bulleted text in two columns.

c. Adjust the size of the placeholder so four bulleted items display in each column.

5. Make Slide 5 active and then insert the **WateringCan** image from your PC4 folder with the following specifications (see Figure 4.8 on page 30):

a. Flip the image horizontally.

b. Change the height of the image to 4 inches.

c. Display the Format Picture task pane with the Size & Properties icon selected and then change the horizontal position to 6 inches and the vertical position to 2.2 inches. Close the Format Shape task pane.

6. Make Slide 9 active, insert a new slide with the Title Only layout, and then create the slide shown in Figure 4.9 (on page 30) with the following specifications:

a. Insert the title *Gardening Magazines*.

b. Create the top shape using the Rectangle: Beveled shape (first column, third row in the *Basic Shapes* section). Change the height of the shape to 1.1 inches and the width to 10 inches.

c. Change the font size to 32 points and then type the text in the top shape. Insert the registered symbol at the Symbol dialog box with the (normal text) font selected.

d. Select and then copy the shape two times. Use the guidelines and Smart Guides to help you align and position the shapes.

e. Change the text in the second and third shapes to match what you see in Figure 4.9.

f. Group the three shapes; apply the Dark Green, Text 2, Lighter 60% shape fill color (fourth column, third row in the *Theme Colors* section); the Olive Green, Accent 1, Darker 50% shape outline (fifth column, last row in the *Theme Colors* section); and the Dark Green, Text 2, Darker 25% text fill color (fourth column, fifth row in the *Theme Colors* section).

7. With Slide 10 active, insert a new slide with the Title Only layout. Type Gift Certificate as the title and then insert a screenshot with the following specifications:

a. Open Word and then open the document named **GAGiftCert** in your PC4 folder.

b. Click the PowerPoint button on the taskbar and then use the *Screen Clipping* option from the Screenshot button drop-down list to capture only the gift certificate in the Word document.

c. With the gift certificate screenshot inserted in the slide, change the height to 3.5 inches and distribute the certificate horizontally and vertically on the slide.

d. Make Word active and then close Word.

8. Make Slide 2 active and then insert a flower icon with the following specifications (see Figure 4.10 on page 30):

a. Click the flower icon located in the *Nature and outdoors* category of the Insert Icons window.

b. Change the height of the icon to 2.8 inches.

c. Apply the Colored Fill - Accent 1, Dark 1 Outline graphic style (second column, third row).

d. Move the icon so it displays as shown in Figure 4.10.

9. Run the slide show.

10. Print the presentation as a handout with six slides displayed horizontally per page.

11. Save **4-Greenspace**.

**Figure 4.6** Assessment 2, Step 2

**Figure 4.7** Assessment 2, Step 3

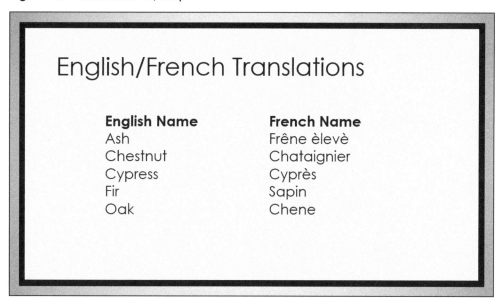

**Figure 4.8** Assessment 2, Step 5

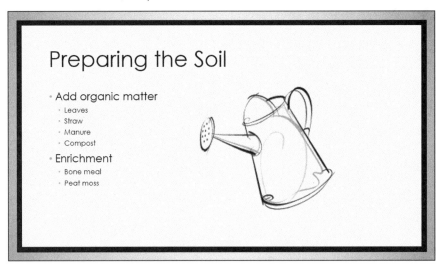

**Figure 4.9** Assessment 2, Step 6

**Figure 4.10** Assessment 2, Step 8

## Save an Image and Insert the Image in Another Presentation

1. With **4-Greenspace** open, make Slide 6 active.
2. Open the **Flowers** presentation and make Slide 2 active.
3. Click the foxglove image and then use the Tell Me feature to reset the picture and the picture size.
4. Determine how to save the image as a picture using the shortcut menu. Save the image in the PNG format in your PC4 folder and name it *Foxgloves*.
5. Close the **Flowers** presentation without saving it.
6. Insert the **Foxgloves** image in Slide 6 of the **4-Greenspace** presentation. Size and move the image so it is positioned attractively in the slide.
7. Run the slide show.
8. Print only Slide 6.
9. Save and then close **4-Greenspace**.

# Visual Benchmark

## Create a Study Abroad Presentation

1. Open a new, blank presentation and create the presentation shown in Figure 4.11 with the following specifications:
   a. Apply the Quotable design theme and choose the purple variant.
   b. In Slide 1, increase the font size for the subtitle to 36 points.
   c. In Slide 2, insert the WordArt using the option in the third column, fourth row (patterned purple fill with purple shadow outline). Apply the Deflate transform text effect (second column, sixth row in the *Warp* section) and size and position the WordArt on the slide as shown in Figure 4.11.
   d. Change the line spacing to double spacing (2.0) for the bulleted text in Slides 3 and 4 and change the line spacing to one-and-a-half spacing (1.5) for the bulleted text in Slide 5.
   e. Insert the **Apartment** image from your PC4 folder in Slide 4. Change the color to Purple, Accent color 1 Light (second column, third row in the *Recolor* section) and size and position the image as shown in Figure 4.11.
   f. Insert the **Colosseum** image from your PC4 folder in Slide 5. Size and position the image as shown in Figure 4.11.
   g. In Slide 6, use the Rectangle: Beveled shape in the *Basic Shapes* section of the Shapes button drop-down list to create the shapes. Change the font size to 24 points for the text in the shapes.
   h. Make any other changes to placeholders and other objects so your slides display similar to what you see in Figure 4.11.
2. Apply a transition and transition sound of your choosing to all slides in the presentation.
3. Run the slide show.
4. Save the presentation and name it **4-RomeStudy**.
5. Print the presentation as a handout with six slides displayed horizontally per page.
6. Close **4-RomeStudy**.

**Figure 4.11** Visual Benchmark

Slide 1

Slide 2

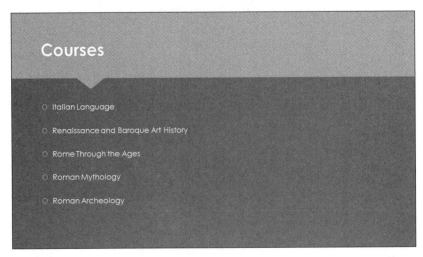

Slide 3

*continues*

Chapter 4 | Review and Assessment

**Figure 4.11** Visual Benchmark—*continued*

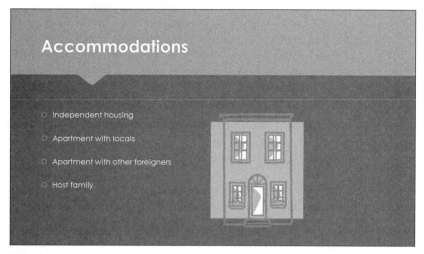

Slide 4

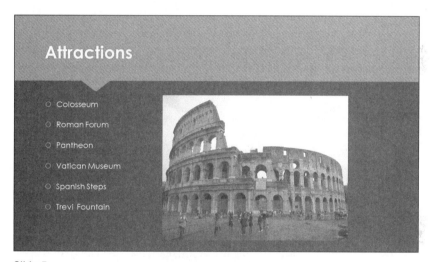

Slide 5

Slide 6

# Case Study

**Part 1**

You work for Honoré Financial Services. The office manager, Jason Monroe, has asked you to prepare a presentation for a community workshop he will be conducting next week. Open the Word document named **HFS** from your PC4 folder and then use the information in the document to create a presentation with the following specifications:

- Slide 1: Include the company name Honoré Financial Services (use the Symbol dialog box to create the é in Honoré) and the subtitle *Managing Your Money*.
- Slide 2: Insert the word *Budgeting* as WordArt.
- Slides 3, 4, and 5: Use the bulleted and numbered information to create these slides.
- Slide 6: Create a text box, set tabs, and then type the information in the *Managing Records* section that is set in columns.
- Slide 7: Create a shape and then insert the slogan *Retirement Planning Made Easy*.
- Include at least one image or icon in the presentation.

Apply a design theme of your choosing and add any additional features to improve the appearance of the presentation. Insert a transition and transition sound to each slide and then run the slide show. Save the presentation and name it **4-HFS**. Print the presentation as a handout with four slides displayed horizontally per page. Close the **HSF** document without saving changes.

**Part 2**

Mr. Monroe will be conducting a free workshop titled *Financial Planning for the College Student*. Create a slide in the **4-HFS** presentation (make it the last slide in the presentation) that includes a shape with text inside with information about the workshop. You determine the day, the time, and the location for the workshop. Print the slide.

**Part 3**

Mr. Monroe would like to post the information about the workshop in various locations in the community and wants to print a number of copies. You decide to copy the shape and then insert it in a blank Word document. In Word, change the orientation of the page to landscape orientation, increase the size of the shape, and then drag the shape to the middle of the page. Save the Word document and name it **4-HFSWorkshop**. Print and then close **4-HFSWorkshop**.

**Part 4**

Mr. Monroe has asked you to locate online finance and/or budgeting resources such as newsletters and magazines. He would like you to locate resources and then create a slide with hyperlinks to the resources. Locate at least two online resources and then insert this information with the hyperlinks in a new slide at the end of the **4-HFS** presentation. Print the slide and then save and close the presentation.

# Microsoft® PowerPoint®

# Unit 1 Performance Assessment

 Data Files

Before beginning unit work, copy the PU1 folder to your storage medium and then make PU1 the active folder.

## Assessing Proficiency

In this unit, you have learned to create, print, save, close, open, view, run, edit, and format a PowerPoint presentation. You have also learned how to add slide transitions and transition sounds to presentations; rearrange slides; customize presentations by changing the design theme; and add visual interest to slides by inserting text boxes, shapes, images, icons, screenshots, and symbols.

**Assessment**

**1**

### Prepare, Format, and Enhance a Conference Presentation

1. Create a presentation with the text shown in Figure U1.1 (on page 37) using the Quotable design theme. Use the appropriate slide layout for each slide. After creating the slides, complete a spelling check on the text in the slides.
2. Add a transition and transition sound of your choosing to all slides.
3. Save the presentation and name it **U1-CSConf**.
4. Run the slide show.
5. Make Slide 1 active and then find all occurrences of the text *Area* and replace them with *Market*.
6. Make the following changes to Slide 2:
   a. Replace the text *Net income* with *Net income per common share*.
   b. Delete the text *Return on average equity*.
7. Make the following changes to Slide 4:
   a. Delete *Shopping*.
   b. Type Business finance between *Personal finance* and *Email*.
8. Rearrange the slides in the presentation so they are in the following order (only the slide titles are shown below):

   Slide 1 = CORNERSTONE SYSTEMS
   Slide 2 = Corporate Vision
   Slide 3 = Future Goals
   Slide 4 = Industrial Market
   Slide 5 = Consumer Market
   Slide 6 = Financial Review

9. Increase the line spacing to 1.5 lines for the bulleted text in Slides 2, 3, 5, and 6.
10. Make Slide 4 active, increase the line spacing to 2.0 for the bulleted text, and then format the bulleted text in two columns with three entries in each column. *Hint: You will need to decrease the size of the placeholder*.
11. Save the presentation and then run the slide show.
12. Print the presentation as a handout with six slides displayed horizontally per page.
13. Display the Reuse Slides task pane, browse to your PU1 folder, and then double-click **CSMktRpt**.
14. Insert the *Department Reports* slide below Slide 4.
15. Insert the *Services* slide below Slide 2.
16. Close the Reuse Slides task pane.
17. Make Slide 8 active, select the bulleted text, and then create and apply a custom bullet using a dollar symbol in a complementary color and set the size to 100%. *Hint: The dollar symbol is located in the (normal text) font in the Symbol dialog box and is character code 0024. (The (normal text) font is the first option in the Font option drop-down list.)*
18. With Slide 8 active, insert the **Money** image from your PU1 folder. Format, size, and then position the image attractively on the slide.
19. Move Slide 4 (*Future Goals*) to the end of the presentation.
20. Insert a new slide with the Title and Content layout at the end of the presentation with the following specifications:
    a. Insert *Future Goals* as the title.
    b. Type International market as the first bulleted item and then press the Enter key.
    c. Copy the bulleted items *Acquisitions*, *Production*, *Technology*, and *Marketing* from Slide 8 and paste them in the content area of the new slide below the first line of bulleted text. (When copied, the items should be preceded by a bullet. If a bullet displays on a blank line below the last text item, press the Backspace key two times.)
    d. Select the bulleted text and then change the line spacing to 1.5 lines.
21. Make Slide 8 active, select the bulleted items, and then apply numbering.
22. Make Slide 9 active, select the bulleted items, apply numbering, and then change the beginning number to *6*.
23. With Slide 9 active, create a new slide with the Blank layout with the following specifications:
    a. Insert the **Nightscape** image from your PU1 folder as a background image and hide the background graphics. *Hint: Do this with the Format Background button on the Design tab.*
    b. Create a text box at the top of the slide, change the font color to White, Text 1, increase the font size to 36 points, and then change the alignment to center.
    c. Type National Sales Meeting, press the Enter key, type New York City, press the Enter key, and then type October 19 to 21, 2021.
    d. Move and/or size the text box so the text is centered above the buildings in the picture.
24. With Slide 10 active, insert a new slide with the Title Only layout. Type Doubletree Guest Suites as the title and then insert a screenshot with the following specifications:
    a. Open Word and then open **HotelMap**.
    b. Click the PowerPoint button on the taskbar and then use the *Screen Clipping* option from the Screenshot button drop-down list to select and capture only the map in the Word document.
    c. With the map screenshot inserted in the slide, apply the Sharpen: 25% correction. Size and position the map attractively on the slide.

25. Insert slide numbers on each slide.
26. Insert a footer for notes and handouts pages that prints your first and last names.
27. Save the presentation and then run the slide show.
28. Print the presentation as a handout with six slides displayed horizontally per page.
29. Close **U1-CSConf**.
30. Close **HotelMap** without saving changes and then close Word.

**Figure U1.1** Assessment 1

| Slide 1 | Title | = | CORNERSTONE SYSTEMS |
| | Subtitle | = | Executive Conference |
| | | | |
| Slide 2 | Title | = | Financial Review |
| | Bullets | = | • Net revenues |
| | | | • Operating income |
| | | | • Net income |
| | | | • Return on average equity |
| | | | • Return on average asset |
| | | | |
| Slide 3 | Title | = | Corporate Vision |
| | Bullets | = | • Expansion |
| | | | • Increased productivity |
| | | | • Consumer satisfaction |
| | | | • Employee satisfaction |
| | | | • Area visibility |
| | | | |
| Slide 4 | Title | = | Consumer Area |
| | Bullets | = | • Travel |
| | | | • Shopping |
| | | | • Entertainment |
| | | | • Personal finance |
| | | | • Email |
| | | | |
| Slide 5 | Title | = | Industrial Area |
| | Bullets | = | • Finance |
| | | | • Education |
| | | | • Government |
| | | | • Production |
| | | | • Manufacturing |
| | | | • Utilities |
| | | | |
| Slide 6 | Title | = | Future Goals |
| | Bullets | = | • Domestic market |
| | | | • Acquisitions |
| | | | • Production |
| | | | • Technology |
| | | | • Marketing |

**Assessment 2**

## Format and Enhance a Kraft Artworks Presentation

1. Open **KAPres** and then save it with the name **U1-KAPres**.
2. With Slide 1 active, insert the text *Kraft Artworks* as WordArt (you choose the style) and apply the following formatting:
   a. Transform the shape of the WordArt.
   b. Change the size so the WordArt better fills the slide.
   c. Change the text fill to a purple color.
   d. Apply any other formatting to improve the appearance of the WordArt.
3. Select Slides 2 and 3 in the slide thumbnails pane and then duplicate the slides using the *Duplicate Selected Slides* option at the New Slide button drop-down list.
4. Change the goal number in Slide 4 from *1* to *3* and change the goal text to *Conduct six art workshops at the Community Center.*
5. Change the goal number in Slide 5 from *2* to *4* and change the goal text to *Provide recycled material to public schools for art classes.*
6. With Slide 5 active, insert a new slide with the Title Only layout with the following specifications:
   a. Insert the title *Clients* and then format and size the title in the same manner as the title in Slide 5.
   b. Insert a text box, change the font to Comic Sans MS and the font size to 20 points, apply the Lavender, Accent 1, Darker 50% font color (fifth column, last row in the *Theme Colors* section) and then type the following text in columns (you determine the tab settings; bold the column heading text):

   | School | Contact | Number |
   |---|---|---|
   | Logan Elementary School | Maya Jones | 555-0882 |
   | Cedar Elementary School | George Ferraro | 555-3211 |
   | Sunrise Elementary School | Avery Burns | 555-3444 |
   | Hillside Middle School | Joanna Myers | 555-2211 |
   | Douglas Middle School | Ray Murphy | 555-8100 |

   c. Select all of the text in the text box and then change the line spacing to 1.5 lines.
7. With Slide 6 active, insert a new slide with the Blank layout, hide the background graphic, and then create the slide shown in Figure U1.2 with the following specifications:
   a. Use the Explosion: 8 Points shape (in the *Stars and Banners* section) to create the first shape.
   b. Apply the Light Green shape fill color (fifth option in the *Standard Colors* section) and apply the Glow: 18 point; Lavender, Accent color 2 glow effect (second column, last row in the *Glow Variations* section).
   c. With the shape selected, change the font to 40-point Comic Sans MS with bold formatting in the Lavender, Accent 1, Darker 50% font color, and then type the text shown in Figure U1.2. Resize the shape if necessary so that the text fits on one line.
   d. Copy the shape two times and position the shapes as shown in Figure U1.2.
   e. Type the appropriate text in each shape as shown in Figure U1.2.
8. With Slide 7 active, insert a new slide with the Blank layout, hide the background graphic, and then create the slide shown in Figure U1.3 with the following specifications:
   a. Set the text in the two text boxes at the left and right of the slide to 54-point Comic Sans MS in the Lavender, Accent 1, Darker 50% font color. Rotate, size, and position the two text boxes as shown in Figure U1.3.
   b. Use the Explosion: 8 Point shape to create the shape in the middle of the slide.

c. Apply the Light Green shape fill color; the Glow: 18 point; Lavender, Accent color 2 glow effect; the Perspective: Upper Left shadow effect (first column, first row in the *Perspective* section); the Lavender, Accent 1, Darker 50% shape outline color; and the 2¼ points shape outline weight.

d. Type the text in the shape and then change the font to 28-point Comic Sans MS, apply bold formatting, and then apply the Lavender, Accent 1, Darker 50% font color. Make sure the text is center-aligned and middle-aligned in the shape. Size and position the shape as shown in Figure U1.3.

9. Create a footer that prints your first and last names and the current date on handout pages.

10. Print the presentation as a handout with four slides displayed horizontally per page.

11. Save and then close **U1-KAPres**.

**Figure U1.2** Assessment 2, Slide 7

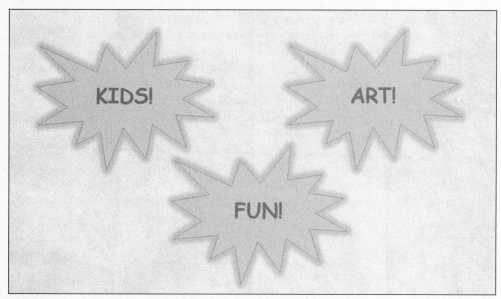

**Figure U1.3** Assessment 2, Slide 8

# Assessment 3    Create and Apply a Custom Theme to a Job Search Presentation

1. At a blank presentation, apply the Dividend design theme and the green variant (third option in the Variants group).
2. Create custom theme colors named with your first and last names that change the following colors:
   a. Change the Accent 1 color to Brown, Accent 6, Darker 50% (tenth column, last row in the *Theme Colors* section).
   b. Change the Accent 2 color to Olive Green, Accent 2, Darker 25% (sixth column, fifth row in the *Theme Colors* section).
   c. Change the Accent 3 color to Orange, Accent 5, Darker 25% (ninth column, fifth row in the *Theme Colors* section).
3. Create custom theme fonts named with your first and last names that change the heading font to Constantia and the body font to Cambria.
4. Save the current theme as a custom theme named with your first and last names. *Hint: Do this at the Save Current Theme dialog box.*
5. Close the presentation without saving it.
6. Open the **JobSearch** presentation and then save it with the name **U1-JobSearch**.
7. Apply the custom theme created with your first and last names.
8. Insert the **Internet** image from your PU1 folder in Slide 5 and then determine the format, size, and position of the image.
9. Insert the **Clock** image from your PU1 folder in Slide 6 and then determine the format, size, and position of the image.
10. Insert an icon of your choosing in Slide 2. Make sure the icon relates to the bulleted text. You determine the format, size, and position of the icon.
11. Improve the visual display of text in all of the slides by increasing the spacing between items and positioning the text placeholders attractively in the slides.
12. Insert the current date and slide number on all slides in the presentation.
13. Create the header *Job Search Seminar*, the footer *Employment Strategies*, and insert the date and page number for notes and handouts.
14. Add the speaker note *Distribute list of internet employment sites.* to Slide 5.
15. Apply a transition and transition sound of your choosing to all slides in the presentation.
16. Save the presentation and then run the slide show.
17. Print the presentation as a handout with six slides displayed horizontally per page.
18. Print Slide 5 as a notes page.
19. Change the slide size to *Standard (4:3)* and ensure the fit.
20. Scroll through each slide of the presentation and make any changes to placeholders and/or images to improve the visual appearance of the slides.
21. Print the presentation as a handout with nine slides displayed horizontally per page.
22. Save and then close **U1-JobSearch**.
23. Open a blank presentation and then delete the custom theme colors, custom theme fonts, and the custom design theme. Close the blank presentation without saving it.

## Assessment 4 — Format and Enhance a Medical Plans Presentation

1. Open **MedicalPlans** and then save it with the name **U1-MedicalPlans**.
2. Apply a design theme of your choosing.
3. Create a new slide with a Blank layout between Slides 1 and 2 that contains a shape with the text *Medical Plans 2021 to 2022* inside the shape. You determine the style, format, position, and size of the shape and the formatting of the text.
4. Change the bullets in Slides 3, 4, and 5 to custom bullets (you determine the picture or symbol).
5. Insert the **Medical** image from your PU1 folder in Slide 4 and then determine the color, size, and position of the image.
6. Make Slide 5 active, and then apply the following formatting:
   a. Select all of the bulleted text and then change the line spacing to 2.0 lines.
   b. With the bulleted text selected, format the text into two columns.
   c. Size and/or move the placeholder so the bulleted text displays attractively in the slide and each column contains four entries.
7. Apply any additional formatting or elements to improve the appearance of the slides.
8. Add a transition and transition sound to all slides in the presentation.
9. Run the slide show.
10. Print the presentation as a handout with six slides displayed horizontally per page.
11. Save and then close **U1-MedicalPlans**.

# Writing Activities

The following activities provide you with the opportunity to practice your writing skills along with demonstrating an understanding of some of the important PowerPoint features you have mastered in this unit. Use correct spelling, grammar, and appropriate word choices.

## Activity 1 — Prepare and Format a Health Plan Presentation

Open Word, open **KLHPlan** from your PU1 folder, and then print the document. Close **KLHPlan** and then close Word. Looking at the printout of this document, create a presentation in PowerPoint that presents the main points of the plan. (Use bullets in the presentation.) Add a transition and transition sound to the slides. Apply formatting and/or insert images to enhance the appearance of the presentation. Save the presentation and name it **U1-KLHPlan**. Run the slide show. Print the presentation as a handout with six slides displayed horizontally per page. Save and then close **U1-KLHPlan**.

Activity
2

## Prepare and Format a Presentation on Saving an Image as a JPG

Open the **KLHPLogo** presentation. Group the image and the text and then save the grouped image as a JPG file named **KLHPLogo**. Close the **KLHPLogo** presentation without saving changes. Create a presentation that includes at least four slides: a title slide, a slide with the steps on how to group objects, a slide with the steps on saving an image in the JPG format, and a slide on the various file formats for saving an image. Format and add visual interest to the presentation.

With the presentation still open, insert the **KLHPLogo** image file in the slide with the steps for saving in the JPG format. Size and position the logo attractively on the slide. Save the completed presentation and name it **U1-JPGPres**. Add a transition and transition sound of your choosing to each slide and then run the slide show. Print the presentation as a handout with six slides displayed horizontally per page. Close **U1-JPGPres**.

# Internet Research

## Analyze a Magazine Website

Make sure you are connected to the internet and then explore the *Time®* magazine website at www.time.com. Explore the site to discover the following information:

• The different sections of the magazine
• The type of information presented in each section
• Details on how to subscribe

Use the information you found on the *Time* magazine website to create a PowerPoint presentation that presents the information in a clear, concise, and logical manner. Add formatting and enhancements to the presentation to make it more interesting. When the presentation is completed, save it and name it **U1-TimeMag**. Run, print, and then close the presentation.

# Microsoft
# PowerPoint

# Unit 2

## Customizing and Enhancing Presentations

# Creating Tables, SmartArt Graphics, Charts, and Photo Albums

 The online course includes additional review and assessment resources.

## Skills Assessment

### Create and Format Tables and SmartArt in a Restaurant Presentation

1. Open **Dockside** and then save it with the name **5-Dockside**.
2. Make Slide 6 active and then create the table shown in the slide in Figure 5.1 (on page 47) with the following specifications:
   a. Create a table with three columns and six rows.
   b. Type the text in cells as shown in Figure 5.1.
   c. Apply the Medium Style 1 - Accent 2 style to the table (third column, first row in the *Medium* section).
   d. Select all the text in the table, center the text vertically, and change the font size to 20 points.
   e. Select rows 2 through 6 and change the font color to Blue, Accent 2, Darker 50% (sixth column, last row in the *Theme Colors* section).
   f. Center the text in the first row.
   g. Center the data in the third column.
   h. Change the height of the table to 3.7 inches and the width to 9 inches.
   i. Horizontally distribute the table.
3. Make Slide 4 active and then create the table shown in the slide in Figure 5.2 (on page 47) with the following specifications:
   a. Create a table with four columns and three rows.
   b. Select the entire table, change the vertical alignment to center, and then change the font size to 28 points.
   c. Merge the cells in the first column, change the text direction to *Rotate all text 270°*, change the alignment to center, change the font size to 40 points, and then type Lunch.
   d. Merge the cells in the third column, change the text direction to *Rotate all text 270°*, change the alignment to center, change the font size to 40 points, and then type Dinner.
   e. Type the remaining text in cells as shown in Figure 5.2.
   f. Change the height of the table to 3 inches.
   g. Change the width of the first and third columns to 1.2 inches.
   h. Change the width of the second and fourth columns to 2.4 inches.
   i. Insert a check mark in the *Banded Columns* check box in the Table Style Options group on the Table Tools Design tab and remove the check marks from the other check boxes in the group.

j. Apply the Light Style 3 - Accent 2 style to the table (third column, third row in the *Light* section).

k. Select all the text in the table and then apply the Turquoise, Accent 1, Darker 50% font color (fifth column, last row).

l. Distribute the table horizontally on the slide.

4. Make Slide 5 active and then create the SmartArt organizational chart shown in the slide in Figure 5.3 with the following specifications:

a. Create the SmartArt graphic with the *Half Circle Organization Chart* option in the *Hierarchy* group at the Choose a SmartArt Graphic dialog box.

b. Select and then delete the second box (select the box containing *[Text]*) so your chart appears with the same number of boxes and in the same order as the organizational chart in Figure 5.3.

c. Type the text in the boxes as shown in Figure 5.3. (Press the Enter key after typing each name.)

d. Apply the Colorful Range - Accent Colors 3 to 4 color (third option in the *Colorful* section).

e. Apply the Polished SmartArt style (first option in the *3-D* section).

f. Apply the Dark Teal, Text 2, Darker 25% text fill color (fourth column, fifth row).

g. Change the height of the organizational chart to 6.5 inches and change the width to 10 inches.

h. Distribute the SmartArt organizational chart horizontally on the slide.

5. Make Slide 1 active and then format the title and create the SmartArt graphic shown in the slide in Figure 5.4 with the following specifications:

a. Create the SmartArt graphic with the *Linear Venn* option in the *Relationship* group at the Choose a SmartArt Graphic dialog box.

b. Type the text in the shapes as shown in Figure 5.4.

c. Apply the Colorful - Accent Colors color (first option in the *Colorful* section).

d. Apply the Cartoon SmartArt style (third option in the *3-D* section).

e. Change the height of the graphic to 3 inches and the width to 9 inches.

f. Align the SmartArt at the bottom of the slide. (Use the Align button in the Arrange group on the SmartArt Tools Design tab.)

6. Make Slide 2 active, select the bulleted text placeholder, and then convert the bulleted text to a Basic Matrix SmartArt graphic as shown in the slide in Figure 5.5 with the following specifications:

a. Apply the Colorful - Accent Colors color (first option in the *Colorful* section).

b. Apply the Cartoon SmartArt style (third option in the *3-D* section).

c. Change the height of the graphic to 4.5 inches.

7. Apply a transition and transition sound of your choosing to all slides in the presentation.

8. Run the slide show.

9. Print the presentation as a handout with six slides displayed horizontally per page.

10. Save and then close **5-Dockside**.

**Figure 5.1** Assessment 1, Slide 6

**Figure 5.2** Assessment 1, Slide 4

**Figure 5.3** Assessment 1, Slide 5

**Figure 5.4** Assessment 1, Slide 1

**Figure 5.5** Assessment 1, Slide 2

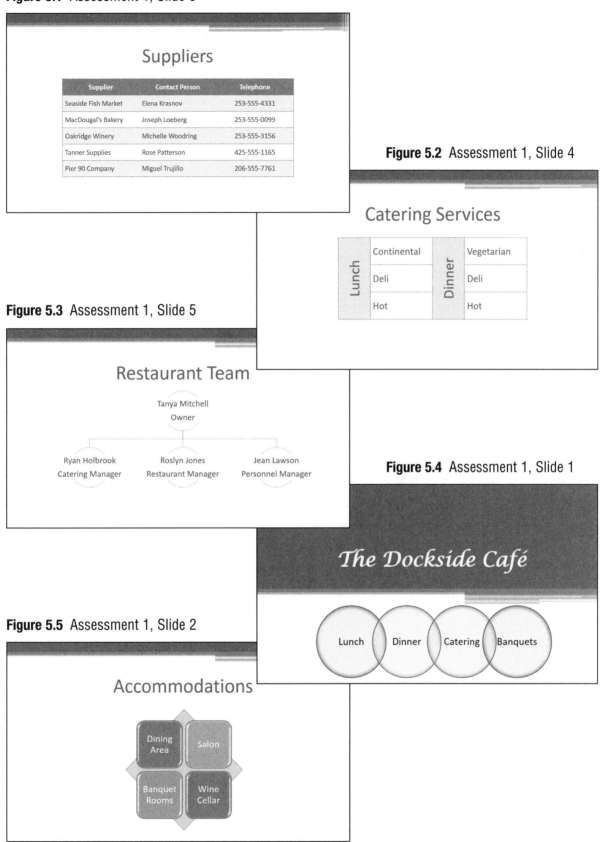

**Assessment**

**2**

## Create and Format Charts in a Marketing Presentation

1. Open **MarketingPres** and then save it with the name **5-MarketingPres**.
2. Make Slide 2 active, insert a new slide with the Title and Content layout, and then create the chart shown in the slide in Figure 5.6 with the following specifications:
   a. Type the slide title as shown in Figure 5.6.
   b. Insert a pie chart and use the *3-D Pie* option to create the chart.
   c. Type the following information in the Excel worksheet:

   |  | Percentage |
   |---|---|
   | Salaries | 47% |
   | Equipment | 18% |
   | Supplies | 4% |
   | Production | 21% |
   | Distribution | 10% |

   d. Apply the Layout 7 chart layout using the Quick Layout button.
   e. Apply the Style 5 chart style.
   f. Move the legend to the right.
   g. Select the legend and then change the font size to 24 points.
   h. Insert data labels on the inside end of the pie pieces.
   i. Select the data labels and then change the font size to 20 points.
3. Print Slide 3.
4. After looking at the slide, you realize that two of the percentages are incorrect. Edit the Excel data and change *47%* to *42%* and change *10%* to *15%*.
5. With Slide 3 active, insert a new slide with the Title and Content layout and then create the chart shown in the slide in Figure 5.7 with the following specifications:
   a. Type the slide title as shown in Figure 5.7.
   b. Use the line chart *Line with Markers* option to create the chart.
   c. Type the following information in the Excel worksheet:

   |  | Revenues | Expenses |
   |---|---|---|
   | 1st Qtr | $789,560 | $670,500 |
   | 2nd Qtr | $990,450 | $765,000 |
   | 3rd Qtr | $750,340 | $780,000 |
   | 4th Qtr | $980,400 | $875,200 |

   d. Apply the Style 4 chart style.
   e. Add primary major vertical gridlines.
   f. Add a data table with legend keys.
   g. Remove the title and remove the legend.
   h. Select the chart area and then change the font size to 18 points.
   i. With the chart area still selected, display the Format Chart Area task pane and then specify a preset gradient fill of Light Gradient - Accent 2 (second column, first row).
   j. Select the Revenues series and then change the weight of the line to 4½ points. (Do this with the Shape Outline button in the Shape Styles group on the Chart Tools Format tab.)
   k. Select the Expenses series and then change the weight of the line to 4½ points.
6. Apply a transition and transition sound of your choosing to each slide in the presentation.
7. Run the slide show.
8. Print the presentation as a handout with six slides displayed horizontally per page.
9. Save and then close **5-MarketingPres**.

**Figure 5.6** Assessment 2, Slide 3

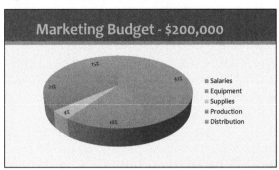

**Figure 5.7** Assessment 2, Slide 4

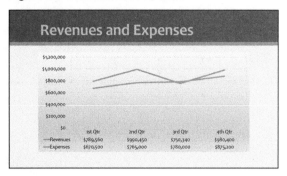

## Assessment 3

### Create a Scenery Photo Album

1. At a blank screen, create a new photo album.
2. At the Photo Album dialog box, insert the following images (keep the Photo Album dialog box open for Steps 3 through 7):

    **AlderSprings**
    **CrookedRiver**
    **MtHood**
    **OregonCoast**
    **LakeEntiat**
    **MtRainier**

3. Rotate the image of Mt. Hood to the right one time.
4. Change the *Picture layout* option to *1 picture with title*.
5. Change the *Frame shape* option to *Simple Frame, White*.
6. Apply the Integral theme.
7. Click the Create button.
8. At the presentation, click the Design tab and then click the fourth variant.
9. Insert the following titles in the specified slides:

    Slide 2    Alder Springs, Oregon
    Slide 3    Crooked River, Oregon
    Slide 4    Mt. Hood, Oregon
    Slide 5    Pacific Ocean, Oregon
    Slide 6    Lake Entiat, Washington
    Slide 7    Mt. Rainier, Washington

10. Make Slide 1 active, select any name that follows *by*, and then type your first and last names.
11. Save the presentation and name it **5-PhotoAlbum**.
12. Print the presentation as a handout with four slides displayed horizontally per page.
13. Close **5-PhotoAlbum**.

## Create a Sales Area Chart

1. Open **5-MarketingPres** and then save it with the name **5-MarketPres**.
2. Make Slide 4 active and then insert a new slide with the Title and Content layout.
3. Use PowerPoint's Help feature to learn more about chart types and then create an area chart (use the *Area* chart type) with the data shown below. Apply design, layout, and/or formatting to improve the appearance of the chart. Type Sales by Region as the slide title.

|  | Region 1 | Region 2 | Region 3 |
|---|---|---|---|
| Sales 2018 | $650,300 | $478,100 | $225,500 |
| Sales 2019 | $623,100 | $533,600 | $210,000 |
| Sales 2020 | $725,600 | $478,400 | $296,500 |

4. Print Slide 5.
5. Save and then close **5-MarketPres**.

# Visual Benchmark

## Create and Format a Medical Center Presentation

1. Open **RMCPres** and then save it with the name **5-RMCPres**.
2. Create the presentation shown in Figure 5.8 with the following specifications:
   a. Create Slide 2 and insert the SmartArt graphic *Hierarchy* (second column, second row in the gallery after clicking the *Hierarchy* option). Apply the Colorful Range - Accent Colors 2 to 3 colors to the graphic. (When typing the text in the SmartArt, press the Enter key after typing each title.)
   b. Create Slide 3 with the SmartArt Basic Radial relationship graphic and apply the Colorful - Accent Colors color and Polished SmartArt style to the graphic.
   c. Create Slide 4 and insert the table as shown in Figure 5.8 (on page 52). Apply the Medium Style 1 - Accent 1 table style and apply other formatting so your table looks similar to the table in the figure.
   d. Create Slide 5 using the information shown in the data table to create the 3-D Clustered Column chart as shown in Figure 5.8. Apply formatting so your chart looks similar to the chart in the figure. As the last formatting step, select the entire chart and change the font size to 16 points and apply the Black, Text 1 font color.
   e. Create Slide 6 using the information shown in the legend and the data information at the outside end of each pie piece to create a 3-D pie chart as shown in Figure 5.8. Apply formatting so your pie chart looks similar to the chart in the figure. As the last formatting step, select the entire chart and change the font size to 16 points and apply the Black, Text 1 font color.
3. Apply a transition and transition sound of your choosing to all slides in the presentation.
4. Print the presentation as a handout with six slides displayed horizontally per page.
5. Save and then close **5-RMCPres**.

**Figure 5.8** Visual Benchmark

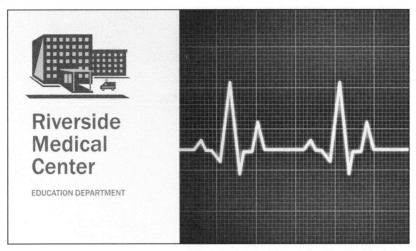

Slide 1

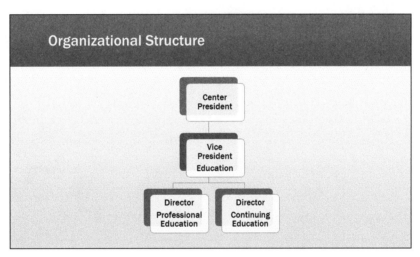

Slide 2

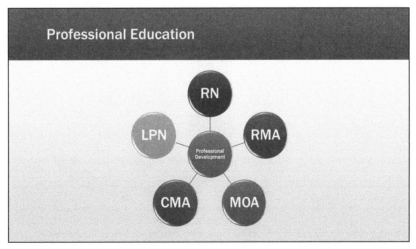

Slide 3                                                                 *continues*

**Figure 5.8** Visual Benchmark—*continued*

## Course Offerings

| Course | Session 1 | Session 2 |
|---|---|---|
| AHA Basic Life Support | October 4 | October 6 |
| AHA First Aid | October 11 | October 13 |
| Basic Cardiac Care | October 18 | October 20 |
| Advanced Cardiac Life Support | October 25 | October 27 |
| Trauma Nursing Care | November 8 | November 10 |
| Emergency Pediatric Nursing Care | November 15 | November 17 |

Slide 4

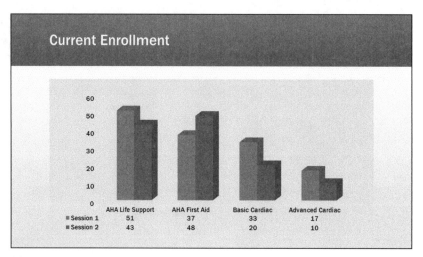

Slide 5

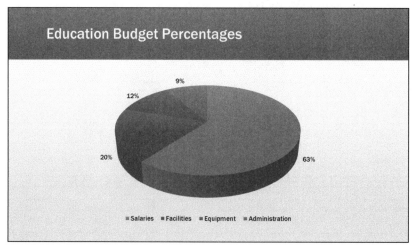

Slide 6

# Case Study

Part

1

You are an administrator for Terra Energy Corporation and are responsible for preparing a presentation for a quarterly meeting. Open the Word document named **TerraEnergy** from your PC5 folder and then use the information to prepare a presentation with the following specifications:

- Create the first slide with the company name and the subtitle *Quarterly Meeting*.
- Create a slide that presents the Executive Team information in a table.
- Create a slide that presents the phases information in a table (the three columns of text in the *Research and Development* section). Insert a column at the left of the table that includes the text *NEW PRODUCT* rotated.
- Create a slide that presents the development team information in a SmartArt organizational chart.
- Create a slide that presents the revenues information in a chart type of your choosing.
- Create a slide that presents the United States sales information in a chart type of your choosing.

Apply a design theme of your choosing and add any additional features or formatting to improve the appearance of the presentation. Insert a transition and transition sound to each slide and then run the slide show. Save the presentation and name it **5-TECPres**. Print the presentation as a handout with six slides displayed horizontally per page.

Part

2

Last year, a production project was completed and you want to display a graphic that illustrates the primary focus of the project. Create a new slide in **5-TECPres** and insert a Funnel SmartArt graphic (in the *Relationship* group) with the following information in the shapes inside the funnel (turn on the Text pane to type the information in the shapes):

> Updated Systems
>
> Safety Programs
>
> Market Expansion

Insert the information *HIGHER PROFITS* below the funnel. Apply formatting to the SmartArt graphic to improve the appearance. Print the slide and then save **5-TECPres**.

Part

3

You have created an Excel chart containing information on department costs. You decide to improve the appearance of the chart and then create a link from the presentation to the chart. Open Excel, open **DepartCosts** from your PC5 folder, and then save it with the name **5-DepartCosts**. Apply additional formatting to the pie chart to make it easy to read and understand the data. Save and then close the workbook and exit Excel. Create a new slide in **5-TECPres** that includes a hyperlink to **5-DepartCosts**. Run the slide show and, when the slide displays containing the hyperlinked text, click the hyperlink, view the chart in Excel, and then close Excel. Print the presentation as a handout with four slides displayed horizontally per page. Save and then close **5-TECPres**.

# Using Slide Masters and Action Buttons

 The online course includes additional review and assessment resources.

## Skills Assessment

**Assessment 1**

### Format a Presentation in Slide Master View and then Save the Presentation as a Template

*Note: If you are using PowerPoint in a school setting on a network system, you may need to complete Assessments 1 and 2 in the same day. Or, you may need to save the template to your PC6 folder and then open a presentation based on the template using File Explorer. Check with your instructor for any specific instructions.*

1. Open a blank presentation, click the View tab, and then click the Slide Master button.
2. Click the top slide master thumbnail in the slide thumbnails pane.
3. Apply the Wood Type theme (the last theme in the *Themes* button drop-down list) and apply the Blue theme colors.
4. Select the text *Edit Master text styles*, click the Home tab and then change the font size to 24 points.
5. Select the text *Second level* in the slide master and then change the font size to 20 points.
6. Insert the **WELogo** image from your PC6 folder in the slide master, change the height of the logo to 0.7 inch, and then drag the logo to the upper right corner of the slide master.
7. Click the Slide Master tab.
8. Click the first slide layout (*Title Slide Layout*) below the slide master.
9. Click the *Footers* check box to remove the check mark in the Master Layout group, which removes the footer and date placeholders from the slide.
10. Select and then delete the slide layouts from the third layout below the slide master (*Section Header Layout*) to the last layout.
11. Preserve the slide master by clicking the top slide master in the slide thumbnails pane and then clicking the Preserve button in the Edit Master group.
12. Click the Close Master View button.
13. Save the presentation as a template and name the template **XXXPublicationTemplate** (use your initials in place of the *XXX*).
14. Close **XXXPublicationTemplate**.

## Use a Template to Create a Publications Presentation

1. Open a new presentation based on the **XXXPublicationTemplate** template presentation (where the XXX represents your initials). (To do this, display the New backstage area, click the *Personal* option, and then double-click the **XXXPublicationTemplate** template thumbnail. If *Custom* displays rather than *Personal*, click the *Custom* option and then click the *Custom Office Templates* option to display the template.)
2. Save the presentation and name it **6-WEnterprises**.
3. Type Worldwide Enterprises in the title placeholder.
4. Type Company Publications in the subtitle placeholder.
5. Display the Reuse Slides task pane, navigate to your PC6 folder, and then double-click **Publications**.
6. Insert the second, third, fourth, and fifth slides from the Reuse Slides task pane into the current presentation and then close the task pane.
7. Insert a second slide master with the following specifications:
   a. Display the presentation in Slide Master view.
   b. Click in the slide thumbnails pane below the bottom slide layout.
   c. Apply the Frame theme.
   d. Click the Frame Slide Master thumbnail in the slide thumbnails pane and then apply the Blue theme colors.
   e. Apply the Style 9 background style.
8. Select and then delete slide layouts from the third layout (*Section Header Layout*) below the new slide master to the last layout.
9. Insert headers, footers, slide numbers, and dates with the following specifications:
   a. Click the Insert tab, display the Header and Footer dialog box with the Slide tab selected, insert the date and time and have it update automatically, and insert slide numbers.
   b. Click the Notes and Handouts tab, insert the date and time and have it update automatically, insert a header that prints your first and last names, insert a footer that prints *Worldwide Enterprises*, and then click the Apply to All button.
10. Close Slide Master view.
11. Make Slide 5 active and then insert a new slide using the Frame Title Slide layout and then type Worldwide Enterprises as the title and Preparing the Company Newsletter as the subtitle.
12. Insert the following text in slides using the Frame Title and Content layout:

Slide 7   Preparing the Newsletter

- Maintain consistent elements from issue to issue
- Consider the following when designing the newsletter
  - Focus
  - Balance
  - White space
  - Directional flow

Slide 8   Preparing the Newsletter

- Choose paper size and weight
- Determine margins
- Specify column layout
- Choose nameplate layout and format
- Specify heading format
- Determine newsletter colors

13. Apply a transition and transition sound of your choosing to all slides in the presentation.
14. Run the slide show.
15. Print the presentation as a handout with four slides displayed horizontally per page.
16. Save and then close **6-WEnterprises**.

## Assessment 3

### Insert Action Buttons in a Gardening Presentation

1. Open **GAPres** and then save it with the name **6-GAPres**.
2. Make Slide 1 active and then insert an action button in the lower right corner of the slide that advances to the next slide.
3. Display the presentation in Slide Master view, click the top slide master in the slide thumbnails pane, create an action button in the lower right corner of the slide that advances to the next slide, and then close Slide Master view.
4. Make Slide 8 active and then create an action button that displays the first slide in the presentation.
5. Make Slide 2 active, click the flowers image, and then create a link to the presentation **MaintenancePres**. *Hint: Use the Action button in the Links group on the Insert tab.*
6. Make Slide 8 active and then make the following changes:
   a. Delete the text *Better Homes and Gardens®* and then type Mother Earth News®.
   b. Select *Mother Earth News®* and then create a hyperlink with the text to the website www.motherearthnews.com.
7. Make sure you are connected to the internet and then run the slide show beginning with Slide 1. Navigate through the slide show by clicking the next action button and open the connected presentation by clicking the image in Slide 2. At Slide 8, click the <u>Mother Earth News®</u> hyperlink. Scroll through the website and click a few different hyperlinks that interest you. After viewing a few web pages in the magazine, close your web browser. When you click the action button on the last slide, the first slide displays. End the slide show by pressing the Esc key.
8. Print the presentation as a handout with four slides displayed horizontally per page.
9. Save and then close **6-GAPres**.

## Assessment 4

### Create an Action Buttons Presentation

1. In this chapter, you learned to insert a number of action buttons in a slide. Experiment with the other action buttons (click the Insert tab, click the Shapes button, and then point to the buttons in the *Action Buttons* section) and then prepare a PowerPoint presentation with the following specifications:
   a. The first slide should contain the title of your presentation.
   b. Choose four action buttons and then create one slide about each of the action buttons that includes the specific name as well as an explanation of the button.
   c. Apply a design theme of your choosing to the presentation.
2. Save the presentation and name it **6-ActionButtons**.
3. Print the presentation as a handout with six slides displayed horizontally per page.
4. Close **6-ActionButtons**.

## Create a Summary Slide in a Design and Production Presentation

1. Open **DesignPres** and save it with the name **6-DesignPres**.
2. Create the following sections using the slides and names listed as follows:
   - Slide 1 – *Design and Production*
   - Slide 2 – *Design Brochure*
   - Slide 8 – *Design Newsletter*
   - Slide 11 – *Prepare Publication*
   - Slide 17 – *Colors in Publication*
3. Make Slide 1 active and then use the Zoom button to insert a summary slide. Remove the check mark from the *1. Publication Design and Production* check box and make sure a check mark displays in the *2. Designing a Brochure, 8. Designing a Newsletter, 11. Preparing a Publication*, and *17. Using Color in Publications* check boxes.
4. Type Preparing Publications as the Slide 2 title.
5. Click in the content placeholder and then click the placeholder border that surrounds all four slide thumbnails.
6. Click the Zoom Tools Format tab, change the zoom duration to *00.50*, and then apply the Drop Shadow Rectangle zoom style (fourth option from the left) and the Green, Accent 6 zoom border color (last column, first row in the *Theme Colors* section).
7. Run the slide show beginning with Slide 1. When the summary slide displays (*Preparing Publications*), click the *Designing a Newsletter* slide thumbnail and then view the slides in the section.
8. When the slide show returns to the summary slide, click the *Using Color in Publications* slide thumbnail and then view the slides in the section.
9. When the slide show returns to the summary slide, press the Esc key to end the slide show.
10. Print only Slide 2 (*Preparing Publications*).
11. Save and then close **6-DesignPres**.

# Visual Benchmark

## Create and Format a Company Branch Office Presentation

1. Create the presentation shown in Figure 6.1 with the following specifications:
   a. Apply the Parallax design theme, the blue theme colors, the Arial Black-Arial theme fonts, and the Style 1 background style.
   b. In Slide 1, delete the title placeholder and insert the text shown in the figure in the subtitle placeholder. Insert the **WELogo** image from your PC6 folder and then size and position the logo as shown in the figure. Insert the Go Forward or Next action button in the lower right corner of the slide as shown in the figure.
   c. Display the presentation in Slide Master view and then click the top slide master thumbnail. Insert the **WELogo** image, change the height of the logo to 0.5 inch, and then position the logo in the upper right corner of the slide as shown in Slide 1 of Figure 6.1. Select the text *Click to edit Master title style*, click the Home tab, and then change to the Blue font color. Insert the Go Forward or Next action button in the lower right corner of the slide master as shown in the figure and then close the Slide Master view.
   d. Create Slides 2 and 3 (on page 60) using the text as shown in Figure 6.1.

e. In Slide 4, create the 3-D clustered column chart as shown in Figure 6.1 using the following numbers:

|  | >$25,000 | >$50,000 | >$100,000 |
| --- | --- | --- | --- |
| Under 25 | 184 | 167 | 0 |
| 25 to 44 | 1,228 | 524 | 660 |
| 45 to 64 | 519 | 1,689 | 1,402 |
| Over 64 | 818 | 831 | 476 |

Make any other changes so the chart appears similar to what is shown in Figure 6.1.

f. In Slide 5 (on page 61), insert the Information action button that links to the website www.myclearwater.com and then size and position the action button as shown in the figure.

g. In Slide 6 (on page 61), insert the **Hospital** image from your PC6 folder, apply the Grayscale color (second column, first row in the *Recolor* section), and then position the image as shown in the figure. Insert a Go Home action button over the Go Forward or Next action button.

h. Change the line spacing in Slides 5 and 6 so your slides look similar to the slides in Figure 6.1.

2. Apply a transition and transition sound of your choosing to all slides in the presentation.

3. Save the presentation and name it **6-WEClearwater**.

4. Run the slide show.

5. Print the presentation as a handout with six slides displayed horizontally per page.

6. Close **6-WEClearwater**.

**Figure 6.1** Visual Benchmark

Slide 1

*continues*

**Figure 6.1** Visual Benchmark—*continued*

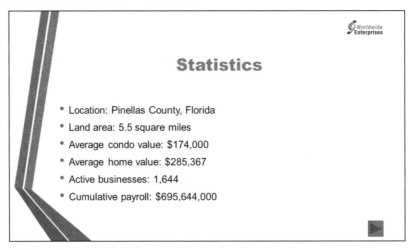

Slide 2

Slide 3

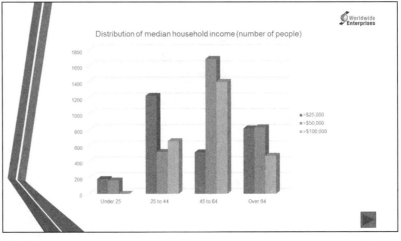

Slide 4

*continues*

**Figure 6.1** Visual Benchmark—*continued*

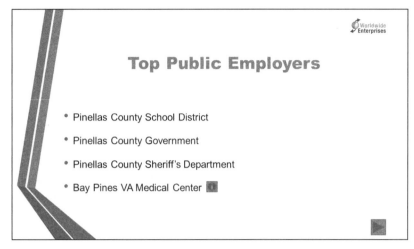

Slide 5

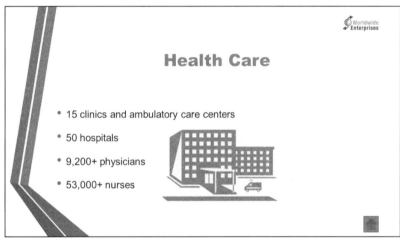

Slide 6

# Case Study

Part

1

You are the training manager for Anchor Corporation and one of your job responsibilities is conducting new employee orientations. You decide that a PowerPoint presentation will help you deliver information to new employees during the orientation. You know that you will be creating other PowerPoint presentations so you decide to create a template with the company logo that can be used to create various presentations. Create a presentation template with attractive formatting that includes a design theme, theme colors, and theme fonts. Insert the **Anchor** image from your PC6 folder in all of the slides. Apply any other formatting or design elements to enhance the appeal of the presentation. Save the presentation as a template with the name **XXXACTemplate** (insert your initials in place of the XXX) and then close the template.

**Part 2**

You have a document with notes about information on types of employment appointments, employee performance, and compensation. Open the Word document named **ACNewEmps** from your PC6 folder and then use the information to prepare a presentation using **XXXACTemplate**. Save the completed presentation with the name **6-ACEmp**. Apply a transition and transition sound to all slides in the presentation, print the presentation as a handout, and then close the presentation.

**Part 3**

Open the Word document named **ACGuidelines** from your PC6 folder and then use the information in the document to prepare a presentation using **XXXACTemplate**. Save the completed presentation with the name **6-ACGuidelines**. Apply a transition and transition sound to all slides in the presentation, print the presentation as a handout, and then close the presentation.

**Part 4**

During the new employee presentation you want to refer to a chart of employee classifications, so you decide to create a link to an Excel workbook. Open **6-ACEmp** and then create a new slide that contains a hyperlink to the Excel workbook named **ACClass** in your PC6 folder. Run the slide show, link to the Excel chart, and then continue running the remaining slides in the slide show. Print only the new slide and then save and close **6-ACEmp**.

**Part 5**

The information you used to create **6-ACGuidelines** was taken from a document that is part of a new employee handbook. You decide that you want to create a link in your presentation to the Word document to show employees the additional information in the document. Create a new slide in **6-ACGuidelines** that includes an action button that links to the Word document named **ACCompGuides** in your PC6 folder. Include other action buttons for navigating in the presentation. Run the slide show, link to the Word document, and then continue running the remaining slides in the slide show. Print only the new slide and then save and close **6-ACGuidelines**.

CHAPTER

# Applying Custom Animation and Setting Up Shows

**7**

 The online course includes additional review and assessment resources.

## Skills Assessment

**Assessment**

**1**

### Apply Animation Effects to a Travel Presentation

1. Open **FCTCruise** and then save it with the name **7-FCTCruise**.
2. With Slide 1 active, click the company logo and then apply the Fade entrance animation. *Hint: Click the Animations tab*.
3. Display the presentation in Slide Master view, click the top slide master layout (*Japanese Waves Slide Master*) in the slide thumbnails pane, apply the Fade animation to the title style, and then close the Slide Master view.
4. Make Slide 2 active and then complete the following steps:
   a. Click in the bulleted text.
   b. Apply the Wipe entrance animation.
   c. Change the direction to From Left. *Hint: Change the direction with the Effect Options button*.
   d. Click in the bulleted text.
   e. Double-click the Animation Painter button.
    f. Make Slide 3 active and then click in the bulleted text.
   g. Make Slide 4 active and then click in the bulleted text.
   h. Make Slide 5 active and then click in the bulleted text.
    i. Click the Animation Painter button to deactivate it.
5. Make Slide 3 active and then insert a trigger by completing the following steps:
   a. Click the banner at the bottom of the slide and then apply the Wipe entrance animation and change the direction to From Left.
   b. Display the Animation Pane.
   c. Click the *Horizontal Scroll* item in the Animation Pane.
   d. Click the Trigger button, point to *On Click of*, and then click *Content Placeholder 2* at the side menu.
   e. Close the Animation Pane.
6. Run the slide show from the beginning and, when the third bulleted item displays in Slide 3, click the bulleted item to trigger the display of the banner.
7. Save and then close **7-FCTCruise**.

**Assessment**

**2**

**Apply Animation Effects to an Employee Orientation Presentation**

1. Open **GEOrientation** and then save it with the name **7-GEOrientation**.
2. Make Slide 2 active and then apply the following animations to the SmartArt graphic:
   a. Apply the Blinds entrance animation effect. *Hint: You will need to click the More Animations button in the Animation group and then click More Entrance Effects.*
   b. Change the SmartArt animation so the sequence is One by One and change the direction to Vertical. *Hint: Do this with the Effect Options button.*
3. Make Slide 3 active and then apply the following animations to the organizational chart:
   a. Apply the Blinds entrance animation effect.
   b. Change the SmartArt animation so the sequence is Level at Once.
4. Make Slide 4 active and then apply the following animations to the bulleted text (click in the bulleted text):
   a. Apply the Zoom entrance animation effect.
   b. Display the Animation Pane and then set the text to dim after animation to the dark blue color (third color from the left). *Hint: Click the down arrow at the right of the Content Placeholder item in the Animation Pane and then click Effect Options.*
5. Apply the following animations to the image in Slide 4:
   a. Apply the Spin emphasis animation effect.
   b. Set the amount of spin for the image to Two Spins and change the duration to 01.00.
   c. Change the *Start* option to With Previous.
   d. Reorder the items in the Animation Pane so the image displays first when running the slide show.
6. Make Slide 5 active, select the SmartArt graphic, and then apply an entrance animation effect so the elements in the SmartArt graphic fade in one by one.
7. Make Slide 6 active and then apply the following animation effects to the images with the following specifications:
   a. Apply the Fly Out exit animation effect to the *Free Education* gift package, change the direction to To Right, and change the duration to 00.25.
   b. Apply the Shape entrance animation effect to the diploma/books image and change the duration to 01.00.
   c. Move the *Free Education* gift package so the bulleted text underneath is visible, apply the Grow & Turn entrance animation effect to the bulleted text, and then move the gift package back to the original location.
   d. Apply the Fly Out exit animation effect to the *Free Toys and Fitness* gift package, change the direction to To Left, and change the duration to 00.25.
   e. Apply the Shape entrance animation effect to the laptop image and change the duration to 01.00.
   f. Move the *Free Toys and Fitness* gift package so the bulleted text underneath is visible, apply the Grow & Turn entrance animation effect to the bulleted text, and then move the gift package back to the original location.
   g. Close the Animation Pane.
8. Make Slide 1 active and then run the slide show.
9. Save **7-GEOrientation**.
10. Display the presentation in Slide Master view, click the top slide master layout in the slide thumbnails pane, apply an entrance animation effect of your choosing to the title, and then close Slide Master view.

11. Make Slide 1 active and then apply the following animation effects:
    a. Click the globe image and then draw a motion path (using the *Custom Path* option) so the image will circle around the slide and return back to the original location.
    b. Apply the Spiral In entrance animation effect to the *New Employee Orientation* placeholder.
12. Run the slide show.
13. Print the presentation as a handout with nine slides displayed horizontally per page.
14. Save and then close **7-GEOrientation**.

Assessment

3

## Apply Animation Effects, Video, and Audio to a Job Search Presentation

1. Open **JobSearch** and then save it with the name **7-JobSearch**.
2. Apply the Wisp design theme and the blue-colored variant (third option).
3. Make Slide 10 active and then insert the **Flight** video file from your PC7 folder. Make the following changes to the video:
    a. Click the Video Tools Format tab and then change the height to 5 inches.
    b. Move the video down so it displays below the title and then distribute the video horizontally on the slide.
    c. Click the Video Tools Playback tab and then specify that you want the video to play automatically (do this with the *Start* option box) and to play full screen.
    d. Click the Trim Video button and then trim approximately the first seven seconds from the start of the video. Click OK to close the dialog box.
4. With Slide 10 active, insert the **AudioFile-03** audio file from your PC7 folder in the slide so it plays automatically, loops until stopped, and is hidden when running the slide show.
5. Compress the video file for HD (720p) quality. ***Hint: This option is located in the Info backstage area.***
6. Run the slide show. After listening to the music for a period of time, end the slide show.
7. Print only Slide 10.
8. Create a custom slide show named *Interview* that contains Slides 1, 3, 6, 7, and 9.
9. Run the Interview custom slide show.
10. Print the Interview custom slide show as a handout with all slides displayed horizontally on one page.
11. Edit the Interview custom slide show by removing Slide 2.
12. Print the Interview custom slide show again as a handout with all slides displayed horizontally on one page.
13. Save and then close **7-JobSearch**.

Assessment

4

## Insert a Video File from YouTube

1. Open **JamaicaTour** and then save it with the name **7-JamaicaTour**.
2. Make Slide 7 active, select the seashell image, create a motion path that travels over the title and ends at the right side of the title. (Consider making the motion path a gentle wave motion and increase the duration time. Double-click the mouse to end the custom path.) Change the *Start* option to *With Previous*.
3. With Slide 7 still active, insert a YouTube video using the key words *Jamaica beaches*. With the video inserted in Slide 7, size the video so it fills most of the slide below the title.

4. Run the slide show and play the video when Slide 7 displays (after the seashell follows the motion path).
5. Print Slide 7 of the presentation.
6. Save and then close **7-JamaicaTour**.

# Visual Benchmark

## Create and Format a Medical Center Presentation

1. Open **RMCPres** and then save it with the name **7-RMCPres**.
2. Create the presentation shown in Figure 7.1 with the following specifications:
   a. In Slide 2, change the image color and size, and position the image as shown in the figure.
   b. Create the SmartArt in Slide 3 using the Staggered Process graphic (in the *Process* section) and apply the Colorful Range - Accent Colors 4 to 5 color to the graphic.
   c. In Slide 4, use the information shown in the legend and the data information shown above the bars to create a Clustered Column chart. Apply the Style 11 style to the chart and add primary major vertical gridlines. Increase the text size of all elements on the chart to 16 points and make any other changes so your chart appears similar to the chart in Slide 4 in Figure 7.1.
   d. Use the Heart shape (in the *Basic Shapes* section) to create the hearts in Slide 5. Apply the Subtle Effect - Red, Accent 1 shape style (second column, fourth row in the *Theme Styles* section) and change the shape outline weight to 4½ pt for all three shapes.
   e. Use the Frame shape (in the *Basic Shapes* section) to create the shape in Slide 6. Type the text in the shape as shown in the figure and change the font size to 28 points.
3. Apply the following animation effects to items in the slides:
   a. Display the presentation in Slide Master view, click the top slide master layout in the slide thumbnails pane *(Medical Health 16x9 Slide Master)*, apply the Float In entrance animation to the master title style, and then close the Slide Master view.
   b. Make Slide 1 active and then apply an animation effect of your choosing to the subtitle.
   c. Make Slide 2 active, apply an animation effect of your choosing to the image, and then apply an animation effect to the bulleted text.
   d. Make Slide 3 active, apply an animation effect of your choosing to the SmartArt, and then specify the One by One sequence.
   e. Make Slide 4 active, apply an animation effect of your choosing to the chart, and then specify the By Category sequence.
   f. Make Slide 5 active and then apply the Shape entrance animation effect to the heart at the left side of the slide. Using the Add Animation button, apply the Pulse emphasis animation effect. Click the same heart and then use the Animation Painter button to apply the entrance and emphasis animation effects to the middle heart and the heart at the right of the slide.
   g. Make Slide 6 active and then insert the **AudioFile-04** audio file from your PC7 folder to play automatically, loop until stopped, and be hidden when running the slide show.
4. Run the slide show.
5. Print the presentation as a handout with six slides displayed horizontally per page.
6. Save and then close **7-RMCPres**.

**Figure 7.1** Visual Benchmark

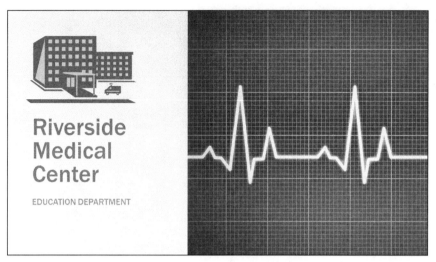

Slide 1

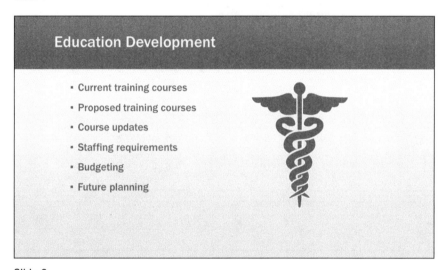

Slide 2

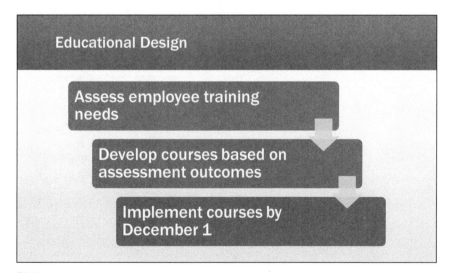

Slide 3

*continues*

**Figure 7.1** Visual Benchmark—*continued*

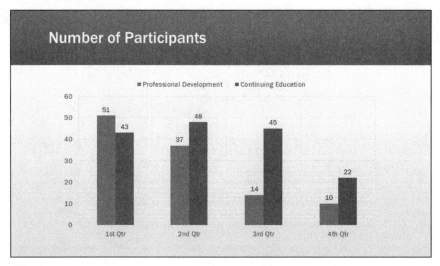

Slide 4

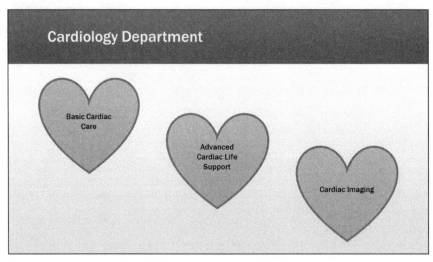

Slide 5

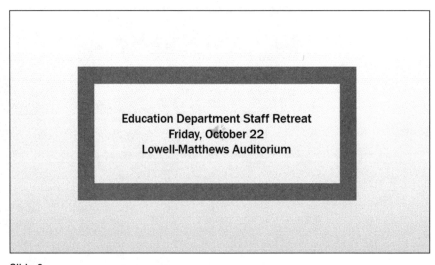

Slide 6

# Case Study

**Part 1**

You are a trainer in the Training Department at Summit Services and are responsible for coordinating and conducting software training in the company. Your company hires contract employees and some of those employees work at home and need to have a computer available. You will be conducting a short training for contract employees on how to purchase a personal computer. Open the Word document named **PCBuyGuide** from your PC7 folder and then use the information in the document to prepare your presentation. Make sure you keep the slides uncluttered and easy to read. Consider inserting images or 3D models in some of the slides. Insert custom animation effects to each slide in the presentation. Run the slide show and then make any necessary changes to the animation effects. Save the presentation and name it **7-PCBuyGuide**. Print the presentation as a handout.

**Part 2**

Some training sessions on purchasing a personal computer are only scheduled for 20 minutes. For these training sessions, you want to cover only the information about selecting computer hardware components. With **7-PCBuyGuide** open, create a custom slide show (you determine the name) that contains only the slides pertaining to selecting hardware components. Run the custom slide show and then print the custom show. Save **7-PCBuyGuide**.

**Part 3**

You would like to insert an audio file that plays at the end of the presentation and decide to find free audio files on the internet. Use a search engine to search for *free audio files for PowerPoint* or *free audio clips for PowerPoint*. When you find a site, make sure that you can download and use the audio file without violating copyright laws. Download an audio file and then insert it in the last slide in your presentation. Set up the audio file to play after all of the elements display on the slide. Save **7-PCBuyGuide**.

**Part 4**

You decide to improve the appearance of the computer buying guide presentation by adding a 3D model and applying the Morph transition to better display different components of a computer. Create three new slides at the end of the presentation, locate and insert a 3D model of a personal computer, and then copy it to the three new slides. In each slide, describe one component of the computer and then rotate or tilt the image to display the component described in the slide. Apply the Morph transition to the presentation and then set all slides in the presentation to transition after three seconds. Run the slide show and make any necessary adjustments to the 3D model. Save and then close **7-PCBuyGuide**.

CHAPTER

# Integrating, Sharing, and Protecting Presentations

8

 The online course includes additional review and assessment resources.

## Skills Assessment

**Assessment**

**1**

### Copy Word and Excel Data into a Sales Conference Presentation

1. Open **NWPres** and then save it with the name **8-NWPres**.
2. Make Slide 2 active and then complete the following steps:
   a. Open Excel and then open the workbook named **SalesProj**.
   b. Copy the chart and paste it into Slide 2.
   c. Size the chart so it fills most of the slide below the title.
   d. Make Excel active, close the workbook, and then close Excel.
3. Make Slide 4 active and then complete the following steps:
   a. Draw a text box in the slide.
   b. Open Word and then open **HerbRemedies**.
   c. Copy the first three terms and the paragraph below each term in the document and paste them in the text box in Slide 4.
   d. Move and/or size the text box so it fills most of the slide below the title.
4. Make Slide 5 active and then complete the following steps:
   a. Draw a text box in the slide.
   b. Make the Word document named **HerbRemedies** active.
   c. Copy the last two terms and the paragraph below each term in the document and paste them in the text box in Slide 5.
   d. Move and/or size the text box so it fills most of the slide below the title.
5. Make Word active, close **HerbRemedies**, and then close Word.
6. With PowerPoint active, apply animation effects to each item on each slide.
7. Run the slide show.
8. Save **8-NWPres**.
9. Print the presentation as a handout with six slides displayed horizontally per page.
10. Export the presentation to a Word document that prints blank lines next to slides.
11. Save the Word document and name it **8-NWPresHandout**.
12. Print and then close **8-NWPresHandout**, and then close Word.
13. In PowerPoint, close **8-NWPres**.

**Copy and Link Word and Excel Data into a Communications Presentation**

1. Open **CommPres** and then save it with the name **8-CommPres**.
2. Open Word and then open **VerbalSkills** from your PC8 folder.
3. Copy the table and embed it into Slide 5. (Hint: Use the the Paste Special dialog box and click *Microsoft Word Document Object* in the *As* list box.)
4. Size the table so it better fills the slide.
5. Make Word active, close **VerbalSkills**, and then close Word.
6. Open Excel, open the workbook named **NVCues**, and then save it with the name **8-NVCues**.
7. Copy the chart and link it to Slide 6. Size the chart so it fills most of the slide below the title.
8. Save and then close **8-CommPres**.
9. Make the following changes to the chart in the Excel file **8-NVCues**:
   a. Change the amount in cell B2 from *35%* to *38%*.
   b. Change the amount in cell B3 from *25%* to *22%*.
10. Save and then close **8-NVCues** and then close Excel.
11. In PowerPoint, open **8-CommPres**. (At the message that displays when you open the presentation, click the Update Links button.)
12. Make Slide 2 active and then type the following comment after the second bulleted item: Ask Lauren to provide a specific communication example.
13. Make Slide 4 active and then type the following comment after the third bulleted item: Insert a link here to the writing presentation prepared by Sylvia.
14. Make Slide 8 active and then type the following comment after the third bulleted item: Distribute evaluation forms to audience.
15. Run the slide show.
16. Save the presentation and then print the presentation as a handout with four slides displayed horizontally per page and make sure the comments print.
17. Run the document inspector and remove comments.
18. Run the accessibility checker. Create alt text for the table in Slide 5 by typing verbal communication skills table in the description text box in the Alt Text task pane. Create alt text for the chart in Slide 6 by typing Pie chart showing the percentage of top five nonverbal cues: Eye contact 38%, Smiling 22%, Posture 15%, Position 15%, and Gestures 10% in the description text box in the Alt Text task pane.
19. Close the Alt Text task pane and the Accessibility Checker task pane.
20. Save and then close **8-CommPres**.

**Save a Sales Conference Presentation in Various Formats**

1. Open **8-NWPres** and then save the presentation in the PowerPoint 97-2003 Presentation file format and name the presentation **8-NWPres-2003format**. (At the Compatibility Checker dialog box, click the Continue button.)
2. Close **8-NWPres-2003format**.
3. Open **8-NWPres** and then save all slides in the presentation as JPEG image files in your PC8 folder. (Or any other location where you are saving your presentations. PowerPoint will automatically create the *8-NWPres* folder with the slide images in it.)
4. Close **8-NWPres** without saving the changes.

5. Open Word and, at a blank document, complete the following steps:
   a. Change the font to Century Gothic, change the font size to 24 points, change the alignment to center, and then type Nature's Way.
   b. Press the Enter key and then insert the **Slide4** image from the 8-NWPres folder. (Use the Pictures button on the Insert tab to insert this slide image.)
   c. Change the height of the slide to 2.8 inches.
   d. Press Ctrl + End, press the Enter key, and then insert the **Slide5** image from the 8-NWPres folder.
   e. Change the height of the slide to 2.8 inches.
   f. Save the Word document and name it **8-Herbs**.
   g. Print and then close **8-Herbs** and then close Word.
6. Open **8-NWPres** and then save the presentation as a PDF file. When the presentation displays in Adobe Acrobat Reader, scroll through the presentation and then close Adobe Acrobat Reader.
7. In PowerPoint, close **8-NWPres**.
8. Capture an image of the Open dialog box and insert the image in a PowerPoint slide by completing the following steps:
   a. Press Ctrl + N to display a new blank presentation.
   b. Click the Layout button in the Slides group on the Home tab and then click the *Blank* layout at the drop-down list.
   c. Press Ctrl + F12 to display the Open dialog box.
   d. At the Open dialog box, make sure the folder containing the Assessment 3 files, such as your PC8 folder (or any other location where you are saving presentations), is the active folder.
   e. Click the option box to the right of the *File name* text box (option box that contains the text *All PowerPoint Presentations*) and then click *All Files* at the drop-down list.
   f. Click the Change your view button arrow below the search text box in the Open dialog box, and then click *List* at the drop-down list.
   g. Make sure that all of your project and assessment files are visible. You may need to size the dialog box to see the files.
   h. Press and hold down the Alt key, press the Print Screen key, and then release the Alt key. (This captures an image of the Open dialog box. You many need to press and hold down the Alt key, the FN key, and then press the Print Screen key.)
   i. Click the Cancel button to close the Open dialog box.
   j. Click the Paste button. (This inserts the image of the Open dialog box into the slide.)
9. Print the slide as a full-page slide.
10. Close the presentation without saving it.

Assessment
4

**Download and Fill in an Award Certificate**

1. Create the certificate shown in Figure 8.1 with the following specifications:
   a. In PowerPoint, display the New backstage area, click in the search text box, type certificate of excellence, and then press the Enter key. Download the *Certificate of excellence for student* template. (If the template is not available at the New backstage area, open the **Certificate** presentation from your PC8 folder.)
   b. Insert the information in the certificate as shown in Figure 8.1.
2. Save the certificate and name it **8-Certificate**.
3. Print and then close **8-Certificate**.

**Figure 8.1** Assessment 4

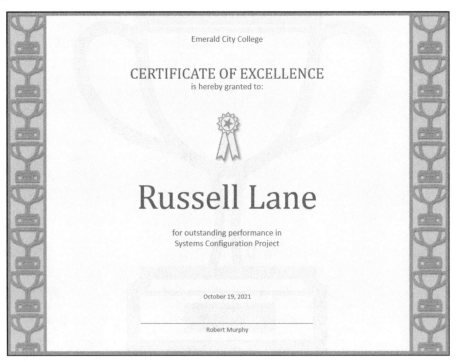

## Visual Benchmark

### Create JPEG Image Files and a Word Document

1. Open **FCTTours**, save all of the slides in the presentation in the JPEG graphic format in your PC8 folder. (Or any other location where you are saving your presentations. PowerPoint will automatically create the FCTTours folder with the slide images in it.) Close **FCTTours** without saving the changes.
2. Open Word and, at a blank document, create the document shown in Figure 8.2 with the following specifications:
    a. Set the two lines of text in 24-point Calibri bold.
    b. Insert each slide and change the height of each slide to 2.5 inches, change the text wrapping to *Tight*, and size and position the slides as shown in Figure 8.2.
3. Save the completed Word document and name it **8-FCTCovers**.
4. Print and then close **8-FCTCovers** and then close Word.

**Figure 8.2** Visual Benchmark 1

# First Choice Travel

## Proposed Tour Package Covers

## Activity 2

### Create a Travel Company Presentation

1. In PowerPoint, download the template named *Cloud skipper design slides* and then save it with the name **8-FCTQtrlyPres**. (If this template is not available online, open the **CloudSkipper** template from your PC8 folder and then save it with the name **8-FCTQtrlyPres**.)

2. Create the presentation shown in Figure 8.3 with the following specifications:
   a. Delete all of the slides in the presentation.
   b. Use the Word outline document **FCTQtrlyMtg** to create the slides in the presentation. *Hint: Use the **Slides from Outline** option at the New Slide button drop-down list.*
   c. Insert a new slide at the beginning of the presentation using the Blank layout and then insert the **FCTLogo** image. (See the first slide in Figure 8.3.) Make the white background of the logo transparent. (Do this with the *Set Transparent Color* option from the Color button drop-down gallery on the Picture Tools Format tab.) Size and position the logo as shown in Figure 8.3.
   d. Make Slide 5 active and then apply the Title Only layout. Open the Excel workbook **Bookings** and then save the workbook and name it **8-Bookings**. Copy and link the chart in **8-Bookings** to Slide 5. Size and position the chart as shown in Figure 8.3. (Close Excel after inserting the chart.)

3. Print the presentation as a handout with six slides displayed horizontally per page.

4. Save and then close **8-FCTQtrlyPres**.

5. Open Excel, open the Excel file **8-Bookings**, and then make the following changes to the data in the specified cells:

   > C2: Change *45* to *52*
   > C3: Change *36* to *41*
   > C4: Change *24* to *33*
   > C5: Change *19* to *25*

6. After making the changes, save and then close **8-Bookings**, and then close Excel.

7. Open **8-FCTQtrlyPres** and update the links.

8. Print Slide 5.

9. Save and then close **8-FCTQtrlyPres**.

**Figure 8.3** Visual Benchmark 2

Slide 1

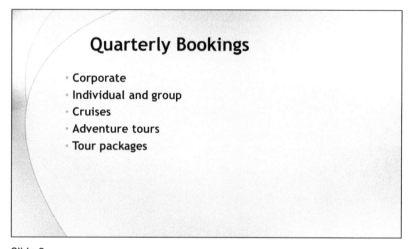

Slide 2

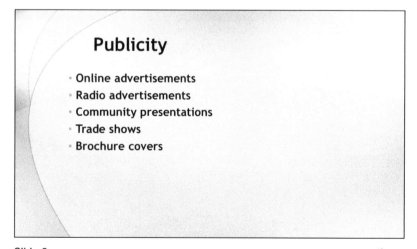

Slide 3

*continues*

**Figure 8.3** Visual Benchmark 2—*continued*

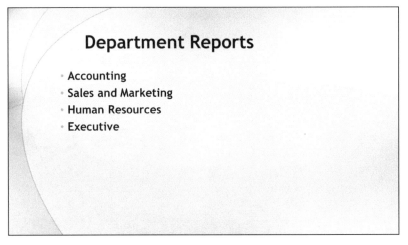

Slide 4

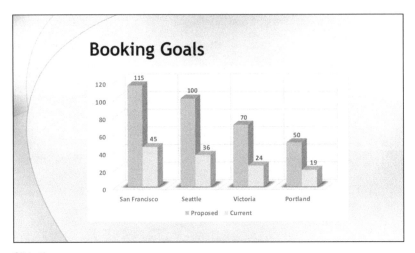

Slide 5

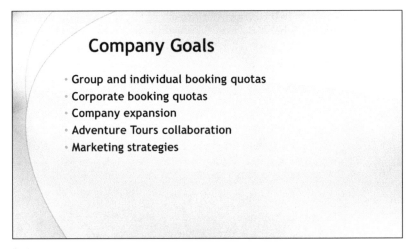

Slide 6

# Case Study

Part

1

You work for Rocky Mountain Family Medicine and are responsible for preparing education and training materials and publications for the center. You want to be able to insert the center logo in publications so you decide to save the logo as a graphic image. To do this, open the one-slide presentation named **RMFMLogo** and then save the slide as a JPEG graphic image. Close **RMFMLogo** without saving changes.

Part

2

You are responsible for presenting information on childhood diseases at an education class at a local community center. Open the Word document named **ChildDiseases** from your PC8 folder and then use the information to create a presentation with the following specifications:

- Open **RMFMDesign** and then save the presentation with the name **8-RMFMDiseases**.
- Use the Title Only layout for the first slide, type an appropriate title for the presentation, and then insert the image named **RMFMLogo** in the first slide. Set transparent color to the background of the logo image. (Do this with the *Set Transparent Color* option from the Color button drop-down gallery on the Picture Tools Format tab.) Size and position the logo attractively on the slide.
- Create additional slides with the information in the Word document named **ChildDiseases**.
- Apply any additional enhancements to improve the presentation. (Consider using the **Temperature**, **Doctor**, or **Sick** image files from your PC8 folder.)

Save the presentation and then run the slide show. Print the presentation as a handout with six slides displayed horizontally per page and then close the presentation.

Part

3

You need to prepare a presentation for an upcoming education and training meeting. Open **RMFMDesign** and then save the presentation with the name **8-RMFMClasses**. Import the Word outline document named **RMFMOutline** and then make the following changes:

- Create the first slide with the Title Only layout, insert the image **RMFMLogo**, and then format, size, and position the logo in the same manner as the first slide in **8-RMFMDiseases**. Insert the title *Education and Training* in the title placeholder.
- Apply the Title Only layout to the *Community Contacts* slide and then copy the table from the Word document **RMFMContacts** in your PC8 folder and paste it into the *Community Contacts* slide. Increase the size of the table so it better fills the slide. (Make Word active and then close the document and close Word.)
- Apply the Title Only layout to the *Current Enrollment* slide. Open Excel, open **RMFMEnroll** from your PC8 folder and then save it with the name **8-RMFMEnroll**. Copy the chart in the workbook and then link it to the *Current Enrollment* slide. (Make Excel active and then close the workbook.)
- Apply any additional enhancements to improve the presentation.

Save the presentation and then run the slide show. Print the presentation as a handout with six slides displayed horizontally per page and then close the presentation. You check the enrollments for classes and realize that more people have enrolled, so you need to update the numbers in the Excel workbook. Open the Excel file **8-RMFMEnroll** from your PC8 folder and then change *46* to *52*, *38* to *40*, and *24* to *27*. Save and then close the workbook and close Excel. Open **8-RMFMClasses** and then update the links. Print only the *Current Enrollment* slide and then close the presentation.

**Part 4**

You decide that you want to include information on measles in **8-RMFMDiseases**. Using the internet, search for information such as symptoms, complications, transmission, and prevention. Include this information in new slides in **8-RMFMDiseases**. Run the slide show and then print only the new slides. Save and then close the presentation.

# Microsoft®
# PowerPoint®

# Unit 2 Performance Assessment

 Data Files

Before beginning unit work, copy the PU2 folder to your
storage medium and then make PU2 the active folder.

## Assessing Proficiency

In this unit you have learned to add visual elements such as tables, charts, and
SmartArt graphics; create a photo album; apply formatting in Slide Master view;
insert action buttons; apply custom animation effects; and set up slide shows. You
also learned how to copy, embed, and link data between programs; how to insert
comments; and how to protect a presentation and inspect it for compatibility and
accessibility before sharing it in various formats.

**Assessment**
**1**

### Save and Insert a Slide in JPEG Format, Format a Slide Master, Create a Table and SmartArt Graphics, and Insert Comments

1. Open **GreenDesignLogo**, save the only slide in the presentation as a JPEG
   graphic image, and then close **GreenDesignLogo**.
2. Open **GDPres** and then save it with the name **U2-GDPres**.
3. Display the presentation in Slide Master view and then make the following
   changes:
   a. Click the top slide master thumbnail.
   b. Select the text *Click to edit Master text styles* (in the bulleted section), apply the
      Tan, Background 2, Darker 75% font color (third column, fifth row in the
      *Theme Colors* section), and change the font size to 28 points.
   c. Select the text *Second level*, apply the Green, Accent 1 font color (fifth column,
      first row in the *Theme Colors* section), and then change the font size to 24 points.
   d. Close Slide Master view.
4. With Slide 1 active, make the following changes:
   a. Insert the image file named **GreenDesignLogo**, which was saved in Step 1.
   b. Set transparent color for the logo background (the white background). *Hint:*
      ***Do this with the* Set Transparent Color *option from the Color button drop-*
      ***down gallery on the Picture Tools Format tab.***
   c. Reduce the size of the logo and position it in the white space in the upper
      right corner of the slide above the water image.

5. Make Slide 6 active and then insert the following data in a table. You determine the formatting and positioning of the table and its data:

| Project | Contact | Completion Date |
|---|---|---|
| Moyer-Sylvan Complex | Barry MacDonald | 01/31/2022 |
| Waterfront Headquarters | Jasmine Jefferson | 02/15/2023 |
| Linden Square | Marion Van Horn | 09/30/2023 |
| Village Green | Parker Alderton | 12/31/2023 |
| Cedar Place Market | Gerry Halderman | 03/31/2024 |

6. Make Slide 7 active and then insert the data from Figure U2.1 in a SmartArt organizational chart. You determine the organization and formatting of the chart.
7. Make Slide 5 active and then create a bar chart with the following data. Delete the chart title and chart legend. You determine the formatting and layout of the chart. (Hint: Make sure to decrease the data range to include only columns A and B. To see all the data in column B, double-click the column boundary line between columns B and C.)

| | Revenues |
|---|---|
| 1st Qtr | $25,250,000 |
| 2nd Qtr | $34,000,000 |
| 3rd Qtr | $22,750,000 |
| 4th Qtr | $20,500,000 |

8. Make Slide 8 active and then insert a SmartArt graphic with the *Repeating Bending Process* graphic (found in the *Process* group) with the following information (insert the information in the slides from left to right). You determine the design and formatting of the SmartArt graphic.

Mission Analysis
Requirements Analysis
Function Allocation
Design
Verification

9. Check each slide and make any changes that improve the appearance of the slide.
10. Make Slide 1 active and then run the slide show.
11. Make Slide 3 active and then position the insertion point immediately to the right of the word *Successes* in the slide title. Display the Comments task pane and then insert the comment Check with Marilyn about adding River View Mall to this list.
12. Make Slide 4 active, click immediately to the right of the word *Australia* in the bulleted text, and then insert the comment What happened to the plans to open an office in Sydney?
13. Print the presentation as a handout with four slides displayed horizontally per page and make sure the comments print.
14. Save and then close **U2-GDPres**.

**Figure U2.1** Assessment 1

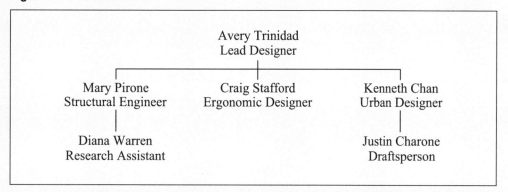

**Assessment**

**2**

## Copy and Paste Data between Programs and Insert Action Buttons in a Travel Presentation

1. Open **NTPres** and then save it with the name **U2-NTPres**.
2. Make Slide 4 active and then create a new Slide 5 (with the Title Only layout) with the following specifications:
   a. Type Extreme Adventures as the slide title.
   b. Open Word and then open **NTExtremeAdventures** from your PU2 folder.
   c. Display the Clipboard task pane. (Make sure the task pane is empty. If not, click the Clear All button.)
   d. Select and then copy *Small Groups*, the paragraph below it, and the blank line below the paragraph.
   e. Select and then copy *Comprehensive Itineraries*, the paragraph below it, and the blank line below the paragraph.
   f. Select and then copy *Accommodations*, the paragraph below it, and the blank line below the paragraph.
   g. Display **U2-NTPres**.
   h. Draw a text box below the title that is approximately 10 inches wide.
   i. Turn on the display of the Clipboard task pane.
   j. Paste the *Comprehensive Itineraries* item in the text box in the slide.
   k. Paste the *Small Groups* item in the text box.
   l. Paste the *Accommodations* item in the text box.
   m. Delete any extra blank lines after the third pasted item.
   n. Clear and then close the Clipboard.
   o. Make the Word document **NTExtremeAdventures** active, close the Clipboard task pane, close the document, and then close Word.
3. Make Slide 1 active and then insert an action button with the following specifications:
   a. Use the *Action Button: Go Forward or Next* option to draw the button.
   b. Draw the button in the lower right corner of the slide and make it approximately one-half inch in size.
   c. Apply the Subtle Effect - Aqua, Accent 2 shape style (third column, fourth row in the *Theme Styles* section).
4. Display the presentation in Slide Master view and then make the following changes:
   a. Click the top slide master thumbnail.
   b. Insert an action button in the lower right corner of the slide with the same specifications as those in Step 3.
   c. Close Slide Master view.

5. Run the slide show. (Use the action buttons to advance slides. At the last slide, press the Esc key.)

6. Create a footer that prints your first and last names at the bottom of each slide. Create a footer for handouts that prints the presentation title *2022 Adventure Packages* and inserts the current date and time on the handout.

7. Print the presentation as a handout with six slides displayed horizontally per page.

8. Save and then close **U2-NTPres**.

## Assessment 3

### Save a Template Presentation and Copy, Embed, and Link Objects between Programs

1. Open the **GSTemplate** presentation.

2. Display the presentation in Slide Master view, insert the **GSLogo** image in the top slide master thumbnail, change the height of the logo to one inch, drag the logo to the lower right corner of the slide master, and then close Slide Master view.

3. Save the presentation as a template (to the Custom Office Templates folder) and name the presentation **XXXGSTemplate**. (Use your initials in place of the *XXX*.)

4. Close **XXXGSTemplate**.

5. Open **XXXGSTemplate**. (To do this, display the New backstage area, click the *Personal* option and then double-click *XXXGSTemplate*. If *Custom* displays rather than *Personal*, click the *Custom* option and then click the *Custom Office Templates* option to display the template.)

6. Save the presentation and name it **U2-GSMtg**.

7. Format the first slide with the following specifications:
   a. Change to the Blank layout.
   b. Use WordArt to create the text *Global Systems*. (You determine the shape and formatting of the WordArt text.)

8. Create the second slide with the following specifications:
   a. Choose the Title Slide layout.
   b. Type 2022 Sales Meeting as the title.
   c. Type European Division as the subtitle.

9. Create the third slide with the following specifications:
   a. Choose the Title Only layout.
   b. Type Regional Sales as the title.
   c. Open Excel and then open **GSWorkbook01**.
   d. Select cells A1 through D5 (the cells containing data) and then copy and embed the cells in Slide 3 as a Microsoft Excel Worksheet Object.
   e. Increase the size of the table so it better fills the slide.

10. Create the fourth slide with the following specifications:
    a. Choose the Title and Content layout.
    b. Type Company Goals as the title.
    c. Type the following as the bulleted items:
       • Increase product sales by 15 percent
       • Open a branch office in Spain
       • Hire one manager and two additional account managers
       • Decrease production costs by 6 percent

11. Create the fifth slide with the following specifications:
    a. Choose the Title and Content layout.
    b. Type Hiring Timeline as the title.

c. Create a table with two columns and five rows and then enter the following text in the cells in the table. (You determine the formatting of the cells.)

| Task | Date |
| --- | --- |
| Advertise positions | 03/01/2022 to 04/30/2022 |
| Review resumes | 05/15/2022 to 06/01/2022 |
| Conduct interviews | 06/15/2022 to 07/15/2022 |
| Hire personnel | 08/01/2022 |

12. Create the sixth slide with the following specifications:
    a. Choose the Title Only layout.
    b. Type Production Expenses as the title.
    c. Make Excel the active program and then close **GSWorkbook01**.
    d. Open **GSWorkbook02**.
    e. Save the workbook with the name **U2-GSExpWorkbook**.
    f. Copy and then link the pie chart in **U2-GSExpWorkbook** to Slide 6. Size and center the pie chart on the slide.
    g. Make Excel active, close **U2-GSExpWorkbook**, and then close Excel.
13. Run the slide show.
14. Create a footer for handouts that prints the presentation title *2022 Sales Meeting* and inserts the current date and time on the handout.
15. Print the presentation as a handout with six slides displayed horizontally per page.
16. Save and then close **U2-GSMtg**.
17. Open Excel and then open **U2-GSExpWorkbook**.
18. Make the following changes to the data in the specified cells:

    B2: Change *38% to 41%*
    B3: Change *35% to 32%*
    B4: Change *18% to 21%*
    B5: Change *9% to 6%*

19. Save, print, and close **U2-GSExpWorkbook** and then close Excel.
20. With PowerPoint as the active program, open **U2-GSMtg**. (At the message that displays, click the Update Links button.)
21. Display Slide 3, double-click the cells, and then make the following changes to the data in the embedded cells (after making the changes to the data, click in the slide to deselect the Excel worksheet):

    C2: Change *2678450 to 2857300*
    C3: Change *1753405 to 1598970*
    C4: Change *1452540 to 1635400*

22. Run the slide show.
23. Print the presentation as a handout with six slides displayed horizontally per page.
24. Save **U2-GSMtg**.
25. Apply a transition and transition sound of your choosing to all slides in the presentation.
26. Use the Rehearse Timings feature to set the following times for the slides to display during a slide show (your actual time will include the duration time and display with an extra second for each slide):

    Slide 1 = 3 seconds
    Slide 2 = 3 seconds
    Slide 3 = 6 seconds
    Slide 4 = 5 seconds
    Slide 5 = 6 seconds
    Slide 6 = 5 seconds

27. Set up the slide show to run continuously.
28. Run the slide show beginning with Slide 1. Watch the slide show until the presentation has started for the second time and then end the show.
29. Save and then close the presentation.

Assessment

4

## Apply Custom Animation Effects to a Travel Presentation

1. Open **NTAustralia** and then save it with the name **U2-NTAustralia**.
2. With Slide 1 active, apply the Fly In entrance animation effect to the subtitle *Australia Tour* that has the subtitle fly in from the bottom.
3. Display the presentation in Slide Master view and then make the following changes:
   a. Click the third slide master thumbnail (*Title and Content Layout*).
   b. Apply a Fly In entrance animation effect to the title that has the title fly in from the top.
   c. Apply a Fly In entrance animation effect to the bulleted text that has the text fly in from the left and then dims to a color of your choosing when the next bullet displays.
   d. Close Slide Master view.
4. Make Slide 5 active, select the sun shape above *Sydney,* and then draw a freeform motion path from Sydney to Melbourne, Tasmania, Adelaide, Perth, Derby, Darwin, Cairns, and then back to Sydney. Change the duration to *04.00.*
5. Make Slide 6 active and then make the following changes:
   a. Click the bottom shape to select it. (You may want to move the top two shapes out of the way.)
   b. Apply the Grow & Turn entrance effect.
   c. Click the Add Animation button and then click the *Shrink & Turn* exit effect.
   d. Click the middle shape to select it and then apply the Grow & Turn entrance effect.
   e. Click the Add Animation button and then click the *Shrink & Turn* exit effect.
   f. Click the top shape to select it and then apply the Grow & Turn entrance effect.
   g. Position the shapes so they are stacked on top of each other so you do not see a portion of the shapes behind.
6. Save **U2-NTAustralia**.
7. Make Slide 1 active, run the slide show, and then make sure the animation effects play correctly.
8. Print the presentation as a handout with all slides displayed horizontally on one page.
9. Close **U2-NTAustralia**.

Assessment

5

## Inspect a Presentation and Save a Presentation in Different Formats

1. Open **U2-GDPres** and then save it with the name **U2-GDPresCheck**.
2. Inspect the presentation using the Document Inspector dialog box and remove comments from the presentation.
3. Run the compatibility checker. (Click OK at the Microsoft Compatibility Checker dialog box.)
4. Save the presentation in *PowerPoint 97-2003* format and name it **U2-GDPres-2003format**. (Click the Continue button at the compatibility checker message.)

5. Close **U2-GDPres-2003format**.
6. Open **U2-GDPresCheck** and then publish it as a PDF file.
7. View the presentation in Adobe Acrobat Reader.
8. After viewing all of the slides, close Adobe Acrobat Reader.
9. Close **U2-GDPresCheck** without saving the changes.
10. Capture an image of the Open dialog box and insert the image in a PowerPoint slide by completing the following steps:
    a. Press Ctrl + N to display a new blank presentation.
    b. Click the Layout button in the Slides group on the Home tab and then click the *Blank* layout at the drop-down list.
    c. Press Ctrl + F12 to display the Open dialog box.
    d. At the Open dialog box, click the option button to the right of the *File name* text box (contains the text *All PowerPoint Presentations*) and then click *All Files* at the drop-down list.
    e. Scroll down the Open dialog box list box to display your assessment files.
    f. Hold down the Alt key and then press the Print Screen button on your keyboard. (This captures an image of your Open dialog box.)
    g. Click the Cancel button to close the Open dialog box.
    h. Click the Paste button. (This inserts the image of your Open dialog box into the slide.)
11. Print the slide as a full-page slide.
12. Close the presentation without saving it.

# Writing Activities

The following activities give you the opportunity to practice your writing skills along with demonstrating an understanding of some of the important PowerPoint features you have mastered in this unit. Use correct grammar, appropriate word choices, and clear sentence structure.

## Activity 1

## Prepare and Format a Travel Presentation

You work for Norton Travel and you are responsible for preparing a presentation on vacations. Open the Word document named **NTVacations** and then print the document. Close the document and then close Word. Using the information in the document, prepare a PowerPoint presentation with the following specifications:

1. Create a presentation that presents the main points of the document.
2. Rehearse and set times for the slides to display during a slide show. You determine the number of seconds for each slide.
3. Insert the **AudioFile-01** audio file from your PU2 folder into the first slide.
4. Set up the presentation to run continuously and the audio to play automatically across all slides and continuously as long as the slide show is running.
5. Run the slide show. (The slide show will start and run continuously.) Watch the presentation until it has started for the second time and then end the show by pressing the Esc key.
6. Save the presentation and name it **U2-NTVacations**.
7. Print the presentation as a handout with six slides displayed horizontally per page.
8. Close **U2-NTVacations**.

## Prepare and Format a Presentation on Media Files

Using PowerPoint's Help feature, learn more about audio and video file formats compatible with PowerPoint. (Use the search text *video and audio file formats*.) Using the information you find in the Help files, create a presentation with *at least* the following specifications:

- A slide containing the title of the presentation and your name
- Two slides that each contain information on compatible audio file formats, including the file extensions
- Two slides that each contain information on compatible video file formats, including the file extensions
- Optional: If you are connected to the internet, search for websites where you can download free audio clips and then include this information in a slide with a hyperlink to the site(s).

Save the completed presentation and name it **U2-AudioVideo**. Run the slide show and then print the presentation as a handout with six slides displayed horizontally per page. Close **U2-AudioVideo**.

# Internet Research

## Presenting Microsoft Office

Make sure you are connected to the internet and then explore the Microsoft website at www.microsoft.com. Browse the various categories and links on the website to familiarize yourself with how the information is organized.

Create a PowerPoint presentation to deliver to someone who has just purchased Microsoft Office and wants to know how to find more information about the software on the Microsoft website. Include tips on where to find product release information and technical support, as well as hyperlinks to other important pages. Add formatting and enhancements to make the presentation as dynamic as possible. Save the presentation and name it **U2-Office**. Run the slide show and then print the presentation as a handout with four slides displayed on each page. Close **U2-Office**.

# Job Study

## Creating a Skills Presentation

You are preparing a presentation to give at your local job fair. Open the Word document **JobDescriptions** from your PU2 folder, print the document, and then close the document and close Word. Use the information in the document to prepare slides that describe each job (do not include the starting salary). Using the internet, locate information on two other jobs that interest you and then create a slide about the responsibilities of each job. Determine the starting salary for the two jobs and then use that information along with the starting salary information for the jobs in the Word document to create a chart that displays the salary amounts. Locate at least two online job search websites and then include their names in your presentation along with hyperlinks to the sites. Save the presentation and name it **U2-JobStudy**. Run the slide show and then print the presentation as a handout with six slides displayed horizontally per page. Close **U2-JobStudy**.

# Integrated Project

This integrated project is a final assignment that allows you to apply the knowledge you have gained about the various programs in the Microsoft® Office suite to produce a variety of documents and files. Complete the project to demonstrate your ability to create documents in Word, build worksheets in Excel, organize data in Access, and design presentations in PowerPoint.

## Situation

You are the vice president of Classique Coffees, a gourmet coffee company. Your company operates two retail stores that sell gourmet coffee and related products to the public. One store is located in Seattle, Washington; the other is located in Tacoma, Washington. The company is five years old and has seen profits grow approximately 10 to 20% over the past two years. Your duties as the vice president of the company include researching the coffee market; studying coffee-buying trends; designing and implementing new projects; and supervising the marketing, sales, and personnel managers.

Activity

**1**

### Write Persuasively

Using Word, compose a memo to the president of Classique Coffees, Leslie Steiner, detailing your research and recommendations:

- Research has shown 10% growth in the past 12 months in the protein smoothie market.
- The target population for protein smoothies is 18- to 35-year-olds.
- Market analysis indicates that only three local retail companies sell protein smoothies in the greater Seattle–Tacoma area.
- The recommendation is that Classique Coffees develop a suite of protein smoothies for market consumption by early next year. (Be as persuasive as possible.)

Save the completed memo and name it **ProjectAct01**. Print and then close **ProjectAct01**.

Activity

**2**

### Design a Letterhead

You are not satisfied with the current letterhead used by Classique Coffees. Use Word to design a new letterhead for the company according to the following specifications:

- Use an image in the letterhead.
- Include the company name: Classique Coffees.
- Include the company address: 355 Pioneer Square, Seattle, WA 98211.
- Include the company telephone number: (206) 555-6690.
- Include the company web address: https://ppi-edu.net/ccoffees.
- Create a slogan that will help your business contacts remember your company.
- Add any other information or elements you find appropriate.

After completing the letterhead, save the Word document and name it **ProjectAct02**. Save the document again with the name **CCLtrhd**. Print and then close **CCLtrhd**.

Activity

**3**

## Prepare a Notice

Using Word, prepare a notice about an upcoming marketing seminar. Include the following information:

- Name of the seminar: Marketing to the Coffee Gourmet
- Location of the seminar: Conference room at the corporate office, 355 Pioneer Square, Seattle, WA 98211
- Date and time of seminar: Friday, October 15, 2021, 9:00 a.m. to 2:30 p.m.
- Topics that will be covered at the seminar:
  - Identifying coffee-drinking trends
  - Assessing the current gourmet coffee market
  - Developing new products
  - Analyzing the typical Classique Coffees customer
  - Marketing a new product line
- Consider including an image in the notice. (You determine an appropriate image.)
- Include any additional company information or details you find appropriate.

After completing the notice, save it and name it **ProjectAct03**. Print and then close **ProjectAct03**.

Activity

**4**

## Create an Organizational Chart

In preparation for an upcoming meeting, you need to prepare an organizational chart of the leadership team at Classique Coffees. In Word, create the following organizational chart using a SmartArt graphic:

Apply formatting to improve the appearance of the SmartArt organizational chart. Save the Word document and name it **ProjectAct04**. Print and then close **ProjectAct04**.

Activity

**5**

## Create a SmartArt Graphic

In addition to the organizational chart, you want to create a SmartArt graphic that illustrates the following steps in a marketing plan:

- Planning
- Development
- Marketing
- Distribution

Apply formatting to improve the appearance of the graphic. Save the Word document and name it **ProjectAct05**. Print and then close **ProjectAct05**.

## Build a Budget Worksheet

Using Excel, prepare a worksheet containing the following information:

**Annual Budget:** $1,450,000

| Department | Percent of Budget | Total |
|---|---|---|
| Administration | 10% | |
| Purchasing | 24% | |
| Sales | 21% | |
| Marketing | 23% | |
| Personnel | 12% | |
| Training | 10% | |

Insert formulas to calculate the total amount for each department based on the specified percentage of the annual budget. After completing the worksheet, save it, name it **ProjectAct06**, and then print it.

Determine how a 10% increase in the annual budget would affect the total amount allocated to each department. With the amounts displayed for a 10% increase, save, print, and then close **ProjectAct06**.

## Determine Sales Bonuses

The Sales Department for Classique Coffees employs seven people. Each employee receives a bonus of 3% of his or her yearly sales if the sales quota is met. The 2021 yearly sales have been calculated and you need to determine the bonus amount, if any, for each salesperson. Using Excel, prepare a worksheet with the following information:

### CLASSIQUE COFFEES
#### 2021 Sales

| Salesperson | Quota | Sales | Bonus |
|---|---|---|---|
| Berenstein | $125,000 | $132,500 | |
| Evans | $100,000 | $95,250 | |
| Grayson | $110,000 | $124,300 | |
| Lueke | $135,000 | $124,750 | |
| Nasson | $125,000 | $147,000 | |
| Phillips | $150,000 | $174,550 | |
| Samuels | $175,000 | $167,825 | |

Determine the bonus amount by writing an IF statement that says if the sales amount is greater than the quota amount, then the salesperson receives a bonus that is 3% of the sales amount. Save the completed worksheet and name it **ProjectAct07**. Print the worksheet, turn on the display of formulas, and then print the worksheet again. Turn off the display of formulas and then close **ProjectAct07**.

### Determine Sales Quota Increases

You have determined that the sales quotas for each salesperson in the Sales Department need to be raised for the upcoming year but are not sure whether the increase should be 5% or 10%. Using Excel, prepare a worksheet with the following information:

#### CLASSIQUE COFFEES
#### Sales Quotas

| Salesperson | Current Quota | Projected Quota |
|---|---|---|
| Berenstein | $125,000 | |
| Evans | $100,000 | |
| Grayson | $110,000 | |
| Lueke | $135,000 | |
| Nasson | $125,000 | |
| Phillips | $150,000 | |
| Samuels | $175,000 | |

Insert a formula to determine the projected quotas at 5% more than the current quotas. Save the worksheet, name it **ProjectAct08A**, and then print **ProjectAct08A**. Insert formulas to determine the projected quotas at 10% more than the current quotas. Save the worksheet and name it **ProjectAct08B**. Print the worksheet, turn on the display of formulas, and then print the worksheet again. Turn off the display of formulas and then close **ProjectAct08B**.

### Determine Monthly Payments

Classique Coffees is interested in purchasing a warehouse in South Seattle and you have identified a warehouse for sale for $800,000. For budgeting purposes, you need to determine the monthly payments for the warehouse. The company is able to provide a 20% down payment and will finance the remaining balance. Using Excel, prepare a worksheet that includes the total price, the amount to be financed (80% of the total price), terms of 15 years (180 months) or 20 years (240 months), and an interest rate of 5% or 5.5%. Use the PMT function to determine monthly payments on the loan for 180 months at 5% and 5.5% and monthly payments for 240 months at 5% and 5.5%. Save the completed worksheet and name it **ProjectAct09**. Print the worksheet, turn on the display of formulas, and then print the worksheet again. Turn off the display of formulas and then close **ProjectAct09**.

### Build a Sales Worksheet and Create a Chart

Using Excel, prepare a worksheet that contains the following information:

| Type of Coffee | Percent of Sales |
|---|---|
| Regular blend | 22% |
| Espresso blend | 12% |
| Regular blend decaf | 17% |
| Espresso blend decaf | 10% |
| Flavored blend | 25% |
| Flavored blend decaf | 14% |

Save the completed worksheet, name it **ProjectAct10**, and then print **ProjectAct10**. With the worksheet still displayed, use the data in it to create a pie chart in a new worksheet. Add the title *Year 2021 Percentage of Sales* to the pie chart and apply formatting to improve the appearance of the chart. After completing the chart, save the workbook (now two worksheets) with the same name (**ProjectAct10**). Print only the worksheet containing the pie chart and then close **ProjectAct10**.

Activity
11

## Build a Projected Sales Worksheet and Create a Chart

Using Excel, prepare a worksheet that contains the following information:

| Type of Coffee | Percent of Sales |
|---|---|
| Regular blend | 21% |
| Espresso blend | 10% |
| Regular blend decaf | 16% |
| Espresso blend decaf | 8% |
| Flavored blend | 24% |
| Flavored blend decaf | 16% |
| Protein smoothie | 5% |

Use the data in the worksheet to create a pie chart in a new worksheet. Add the title *Year 2022 Projected Percentage of Sales* to the pie chart and apply formatting to improve the appearance of the chart. After completing the chart, save the workbook and name it **ProjectAct11**. Print only the worksheet containing the pie chart and then close **ProjectAct11**.

Analyze the sales data by comparing and contrasting the pie charts in **ProjectAct10** and **ProjectAct11**. What areas in the projected sales percentages have changed? What do these changes indicate? Assume that the projected 2022 annual income for Classique Coffees is $2,200,000. What amount of that income will come from protein smoothies? Does this amount warrant marketing this new product? Use Word to prepare a memo to Leslie Steiner that includes your analysis. Add any other interpretations based on your analysis of the pie charts. Save the memo and name it **WordProject11**. Print and then close **WordProject11**.

Activity
12

## Design and Create a Presentation

Using PowerPoint, prepare a marketing presentation. Include the following information:

- Classique Coffees 2022 Marketing Plan (Use this as the title.)
- Company reorganization (Insert the organizational chart you created in Activity 4.)
- 2021 sales percentages (Insert the pie chart from **ProjectAct10**.)
- 2022 projected sales percentages (Insert the pie chart from **ProjectAct11**.)
- Protein smoothie marketing strategy:
  - Target customer
  - Analysis of competition
  - Wholesale resources
  - Pricing
  - Volume
- Product placement:
  - Stocking strategies
  - Shelf allocation
  - Stock rotation schedule
  - Seasonal display

In preparing the slide presentation, you determine the design theme and layouts. Include images to improve the appearance of the presentation and apply animations to all the slides. After completing the presentation, save it and name it **ProjectAct12**. Run the slide show and then print the presentation with six slides displayed horizontally per page.

## Activity 13

### Create a Database and Organize Data

Use Access to create a database for Classique Coffees that contains information on suppliers and products. Save the database as **ClassiqueCoffees**. Include the following tables and fields:

**Suppliers table:**
> *SupplierNo*
> *SupplierName*
> *Address*
> *City*
> *State*
> *ZipCode*
> *Email*

**Products table**:
> *ProductNo*
> *Product*
> *SupplierNo*

Type the following data in the Suppliers table:

| | | |
|---|---|---|
| *SupplierNo* | = | 24 |
| *SupplierName* | = | Gourmet Blends |
| *Address* | = | 109 South Madison Avenue |
| *City* | = | Seattle |
| *State* | = | WA |
| *ZipCode* | = | 98032 |
| *Email* | = | gblends@ppi-edu.net |

| | | |
|---|---|---|
| *SupplierNo* | = | 36 |
| *SupplierName* | = | Jannsen Company |
| *Address* | = | 4122 South Sprague Street |
| *City* | = | Tacoma |
| *State* | = | WA |
| *ZipCode* | = | 98402 |
| *Email* | = | jannsen@ppi-edu.net |

| | | |
|---|---|---|
| *SupplierNo* | = | 62 |
| *SupplierName* | = | Sure Shot Supplies |
| *Address* | = | 291 Pacific Avenue |
| *City* | = | Tacoma |
| *State* | = | WA |
| *ZipCode* | = | 98418 |
| *Email* | = | sssupplies@ppi-edu.net |

| | | | | | |
|---|---|---|---|---|---|
| *SupplierNo* | = | 41 | | | |
| *SupplierName* | = | Bertolinos | | | |
| *Address* | = | 11711 Meridian Avenue East | | | |
| *City* | = | Seattle | | | |
| *State* | = | WA | | | |
| *ZipCode* | = | 98109 | | | |
| *Email* | = | bertolino@ppi-edu.net | | | |

Type the following data in the Products table:

| | | | | | |
|---|---|---|---|---|---|
| *ProductNo* | = | 12A-0 | *ProductNo* | = | 59R-1 |
| *Product* | = | Premium blend | *Product* | = | Vanilla syrup |
| *SupplierNo* | = | 24 | *SupplierNo* | = | 62 |
| | | | | | |
| *ProductNo* | = | 12A-1 | *ProductNo* | = | 59R-2 |
| *Product* | = | Cappuccino blend | *Product* | = | Raspberry syrup |
| *SupplierNo* | = | 24 | *SupplierNo* | = | 62 |
| | | | | | |
| *ProductNo* | = | 12A-2 | *ProductNo* | = | 59R-3 |
| *Product* | = | Hazelnut blend | *Product* | = | Chocolate syrup |
| *SupplierNo* | = | 24 | *SupplierNo* | = | 62 |
| | | | | | |
| *ProductNo* | = | 21B-2 | *ProductNo* | = | 89T-3 |
| *Product* | = | 12-oz cup | *Product* | = | Napkins, 500 ct |
| *SupplierNo* | = | 36 | *SupplierNo* | = | 41 |
| | | | | | |
| *ProductNo* | = | 21B-3 | *ProductNo* | = | 89T-4 |
| *Product* | = | 16-oz cup | *Product* | = | 6-inch stir stick |
| *SupplierNo* | = | 36 | *SupplierNo* | = | 41 |

Create a relationship between the two tables using the *SupplierNo* field in the Suppliers table as the "one" and the *SupplierNo* field in the Products table as the "many." Enforce integrity and cascade fields and rows. Print the relationship report.

Create a form with the Suppliers table (name the form *Suppliers*) and then use the form to enter one more record with the following data: Supplier number 70, Specialty Supplies, 350 Yakima Avenue, Tacoma, WA 98412, specsupplies@ppi-edu.net. In the subdatasheet in the new record, type 95X-6 as the product number and Sugar packets, 200 ct as the product.

Print both the Suppliers table and the Products table in landscape orientation. Create a separate query for each bulleted item listed below:

- Suppliers and products: From the Suppliers table, include the supplier name, address, city, state, and zip code. From the Products table, include the product number and product. Name the query *SupplierProducts*, print the query in landscape orientation, and then close the query.

- Suppliers in Tacoma: From the Suppliers table, include the supplier name, address, city, state, and zip code. Name the query *TacomaSuppliers* and then print and close the query.

- Products sold by supplier number 62: From the Suppliers table include the supplier number and supplier name. From the Products table include the product. Name the query *Supplier62Products* and then print and close the query.

Create a report with the SupplierProducts query. Delete the control object at the bottom of the SupplierName column and the content control containing the text *Page 1 of 1*. Adjust the column widths so the report will print on one page. Save and name the report *SupplierProducts*. Print and then close the report.

Merge the TacomaSuppliers query with the **CCLtrhd** document (created in Activity 2) and then compose a business letter. You determine the inside address and an appropriate salutation. Include the following information in the letter:

- Explain that Classique Coffees is interested in selling protein smoothies in the greater Seattle–Tacoma area.

- Ask if the company offers any protein smoothie products.

- If the company does not currently offer any protein smoothie products, ask whether these products will be available in the future.

- Ask the company to send materials on current products and specifically on protein smoothies.

- Ask someone at the company to contact you at the Classique Coffees by telephone at (206) 555-6690 or by email at ccoffees@ppi-edu.net.

- Include any other information that you feel is appropriate to the topic.

Merge to a new document and then save the document with the name **ProjectAct13**. Print and then close **ProjectAct13**. Save the main document as **SmoothieLtrMD** and then close **SmoothieLtrMD**.

## Activity 14

### Assess Your Work

Review the documents and files you developed and create a Word document assessing your work. To help you develop an objective perspective of your work, openly solicit constructive criticism from your teacher, peers, and contacts outside school. Your self-assessment document should specify the weaknesses and strengths of each piece and your specific recommendations for revision and improvement.